HL
D0277532

Challenging Racism

USING THE HUMAN RIGHTS ACT

Challenging Racism

USING THE HUMAN RIGHTS ACT

Edited by Barry Clarke

Lawrence & Wishart
LONDON 2003

Lawrence and Wishart Limited
99a Wallis Road
London
E9 5LN

First published 2003

Copyright © Discrimination Law Association 2003

The Commission for Racial Equality, The 1990 Trust and the Immigration Law Practitioners' Association. have asserted their right under the Copyright, Designs and Patents Act, 1988, to be identified as the Author of this work.

The support of the Joseph Rowntree Charitable Trust and the Allen Lane Foundation is gratefully acknowledged for assistance in the production of this book.

All rights reserved. Apart from fair dealing for the purpose of private study, research, criticism or review, no part of this publication may be reproduced, stored in a retrieval system, or transmitted, in any form or by any means, electronic, electrical, chemical, mechanical, optical, photocopying, recording or otherwise, without the prior permission of the copyright owner.

British Library Cataloguing in Publication Data.
A catalogue record for this book is available from the British Library

ISBN 0 85315 931 9

Text setting Etype, Liverpool
Printed and bound by Bookcraft, Midsomer Norton

Contents

Foreword

Baroness Howells of St David's, OBE

The last few years have represented an exciting time for human rights and anti-racist activists alike. The Human Rights Act 1998 finally took effect in October 2000. The Race Relations (Amendment) Act 2000 came into force in April 2001 and soon the new EC Race Directive will be implemented.

Of course, human rights and anti-racism are not separate areas. Far from it. Some might say that the long overdue reform of the Race Relations Act 1976 was the result of the Inquiry into the murder of Stephen Lawrence and that the two go hand in hand. Racism is a violation of human rights. The amended race relations legislation is rooted in human rights principles and will continue to play a unique role in community advice agencies and organisations.

But these agencies and organisations require a resource to assist them in their understanding of how the HRA can be used to challenge racism and racial discrimination in the United Kingdom. They need a book that does not overcome them with legalese, but addresses these complicated issues in as accessible a manner as possible. The book you are holding has been prepared with this need in mind. I congratulate the 1990 Trust, the Discrimination Law Association, the Immigration Law Practitioners' Association, and the Commission for Racial Equality on their successful partnership in trying to fulfil this need.

Having been the Chair of a Race Equality Council and active in community anti-racism work for many years, I am particularly pleased to see that the book is targeted at campaigners and lay workers, rather than simply at lawyers. We all know how difficult it can be to tackle racism through the courts. At a time when the government speaks of creating a 'human rights culture', it is important that groups (big and small, lawyers and non-lawyers) are able to work effectively with the law to that end. This means that we must ensure that human rights principles become integrated into the heart of decision-making processes and that all public authorities accept the fact that racism is a violation of human rights. The spirit of both the HRA and the amended RRA will be as important, if not more important, than the precise letter of these laws. And this 'spirit' is rooted in the principles of equality, justice and dignity for all.

This book will be a valuable tool in equipping communities to know their rights and to have their rights upheld. It will play a significant role in ensuring that, as a human rights culture develops in the UK, the anti-racism agenda will not be marginalised as something different or unrelated. Rather, in this 'post-Macpherson period', I trust we are at a time when we will recognise that racist crimes are not simply crimes against black and ethnic groups; they are crimes against humanity, and they are crimes that violate basic human rights.

ACKNOWLEDGEMENTS AND THANKS

The original idea for this book arose as a proposal from a very successful conference, held in October 1998, called 'Making Rights Real'. It was subtitled: 'Using the Human Rights Act to Fight Racism'. The first people who should therefore be thanked for making the book real are therefore all the participants at this conference. The sponsors then took the idea forward and, at long last, here we are!

We would like to thank the *Joseph Rowntree Charitable Trust* and the *Allen Lane Foundation*, who have made this project possible through their generous financial support. In addition, we were positively encouraged in the project by *Stephen Pittam* of the Joseph Rowntree Charitable Trust, to try to ensure that knowledge about the Human Rights Act became available to a non-legal audience, particularly those 'frontline' community organisations advising victims of racism.

We would like formally to thank the four sponsoring organisations – the *1990 Trust*, the *Discrimination Law Association*, the *Immigration Law Practitioners' Association* and the *Commission for Racial Equality* – that worked together to enable the project to be fulfilled. Their representatives on the project group were, respectively, *Veena Vasista*, *Paul Crofts*, *Susan Rowlands* and *Barbara Cohen*.

We would also like to thank all the contributors to the book, who devoted time and energy to writing their individual chapters without any payment whatsoever.

Others who helped with the project in various ways included *Philton Moore*, *Rick Scannell*, *Gay Moon* and *Harminder Singh* (present and past DLA Chair), the *CRE's Press & Publicity section*, *Gaby Charing* (DLA Development Officer), *Sally Davison* (Lawrence & Wishart, our publishers). Without all their support, advice, encouragement and help, the project would not have been as successful as it is.

Finally (but certainly not least), we would like to thank the editor – *Barry Clarke* – who had the task of pulling all the chapters together in as 'lay-reader friendly' style as possible. We know this was extremely time-consuming work and came at a time in this personal life that made this sometimes very difficult. The fact that he persevered is a reflection of his commitment to the project.

Paul Crofts

ABBREVIATIONS USED

CCA	Contempt of Court Act 1981
CDA	Crime and Disorder Act 1998
Convention	European Convention on Human Rights and Fundamental Freedoms 1950
CrimDA	Criminal Damage Act 1971
CJPOA	Criminal Justice and Public Order Act 1994
CPIA	Criminal Procedure and Investigations Act 1996
CPS	Crown Prosecution Service
DDA	Disability Discrimination Act 1995
DPA	Data Protection Act 1998
EA	Education Act 1996
ECtHR	European Court of Human Rights
ECommHR	European Commission of Human Rights
ERA	Employment Rights Act 1996
FOA	Football Offences Act 1991
FHEA	Further and Higher Education Act 1992
HA	Housing Act 1996
HRA	Human Rights Act 1998
IA	Immigration Act 1971
IAA	Immigration and Asylum Act 1999
ICCPR	International Covenant on Civil and Political Rights
ISA	Intelligence Service Act 1984
MCA	Malicious Communications Act 1988
OPA	Offences against the Person Act 1861
ObPA	Obscene Publications Act 1959
PA	Police Act 1997
PACE	Police and Criminal Evidence Act 1984
PFEA	Protection From Eviction Act 1977
POA	Public Order Act 1986
PHA	Protection from Harassment Act 1997
RIPA	Regulation of Investigatory Powers Act 2000
RRA	Race Relations Act 1976
RR(A)A	Race Relations (Amendment) Act 2000
SDA	Sex Discrimination Act 1975
SSFA	Schools and Standards Framework Act 1998
SSA	Social Security Act 1998
SecSA	Security Service Act 1989
TA	Telecommunications Act 1984

EDITOR'S NOTE

It is not intended that this book should be read in one sitting, from beginning to end, although of course readers are free to do so if they wish. Rather, it is intended as a reference book, which can be referred to as occasion demands. It is written is a way that is meant to make it accessible to those who would 'dip into it' from time to time, checking for human rights principles that may be relevant to a particular case.

It should be made very clear at the outset that this is not designed to be a legal textbook, and it is not designed for lawyers. There are far better books with detailed statutory and case law references for those who wish to carry out detailed legal research. Instead, it is designed as a readable guide that prompts lateral thinking, or as a 'first port of call', in either case for the lay adviser. The hope is that the book equips its readers with a sense of how best to use human rights principles to challenge racism and racial discrimination. Its tone of encouragement in parts is properly balanced in others by the need to exercise caution. The HRA is not a panacea, and the courts have made clear that they will give short shrift to those who try to use it as such without properly reasoned argument.

Statutory and case law references have therefore been kept to an absolute minimum, so as not to deter the lay audience at which this book is targeted. Efforts have also been made to minimise duplication between chapters, although numerous practical points are common to many areas of law that are examined in the book. An obvious example of this is the parasitic nature of Article 14, a key point that features time and again throughout this book. For convenience, legislation is referred to by acronym – e.g. RRA for Race Relations Act 1976, HRA for Human Rights Act 1998 – and a list of abbreviations used is on the preceding page.

The book is thematic in nature. That is, Articles of the Convention are not examined in turn. Rather, it deals with each of the subject areas that are most likely to concern lay advisers, such as housing, immigration, employment, education, social welfare, police powers, and so on. Many of the lay advisers at whom this book is targeted with already have some experience in dealing with some of these subject areas. Where they may lack experience, however, is in dealing with these same subjects in the new context that exists since the Human Rights Act 1998 came into force.

In response to that perceived need, therefore, most of these subjects have been examined in two contexts: the pre-HRA framework (i.e. the law as it was) and the post-HRA framework (i.e. the law as it now is, or as it may become). The only slight complication to this approach is in connection with the RR(A)A, which came into force after the HRA but may be most easily examined (albeit without chronological accuracy) as part of the pre-HRA framework.

To avoid misleading any readers, it is important to emphasise that, in most cases, the pre-HRA framework remains, but has been modified to a greater or lesser extent by the provisions of the HRA. The most relevant Articles to that subject area are then examined, followed by a case study. To underline the practical approach of the book, there are further chapters on funding, campaigning and using the media.

Advisers dealing with one or two of these specific subject areas should still take the opportunity to read the excellent introductory chapters by Razia Karim and Barbara Cohen. They contain useful guidance to which it is helpful to keep returning, on human rights and race discrimination respectively.

Where expressed, opinions are those of the individual contributors, and they alone are responsible for them. They are not the responsibility of other contributors, the editor or the book's sponsors.

The law as described is applicable to England and Wales, and correctly stated up to September 2002. Although some of the book will be relevant in Scotland and Northern Ireland, it is not intended to be applicable to those jurisdictions.

This book provides general guidance only and does not contain specific legal advice. If readers have a particular legal question, they should take separate legal advice.

Barry Clarke

Introduction to the
Human Rights Act 1998

Razia Karim

The enactment of the HRA in October 2000 represented a positive and exciting development for human rights in the UK. For the first time, all people in the UK were guaranteed a set of human rights enforceable in domestic courts. These rights are based on the Convention, the bulk of which is incorporated by the HRA.

Human rights are important. They are the expression of belief in the values of democracy, peace and justice and of respect for the dignity and worth of each individual. Human rights protect the individual from abuse of power by the state while seeking a balance between the rights and responsibilities of citizens. They are therefore an important part of citizenship.

For all minorities, human rights are necessary. The emphasis of human rights is on individual rights and not those of the majority or most influential groups. The majority view – or public interest – is not ignored; but human rights law seeks a proper balance between the public interest and the rights of the individual. Respect for individual rights ensures the protection of minorities and their effective participation in society.

The principle of non-discrimination is a central theme in human rights law and provides a legal base for arguing that racism itself may be a violation of fundamental human rights and freedoms.

The impact of the HRA has affected:

- **Individuals**
  Individuals can assert Convention rights in UK courts and tribunals.
- **Public authorities**
  It is unlawful for public authorities to act incompatibly with the HRA and they will be held accountable if they do.

- **Courts and tribunals**
  Courts and tribunals have begun to develop their own human rights case law for the UK.
- **Legislation**
  Legislation must be interpreted and given effect as far as possible consistent with the Convention.
- **Parliament**
  The Government must certify that future legislation and policy is compatible with the HRA.

This chapter is intended to serve as a general introduction to the HRA. It aims to provide a reference point for the entire book. As stated in the Editor's Note, it introduces concepts that will be referred to in detail in subsequent chapters, with the hope of minimising any duplication with those chapters. There is first an overview of the Convention, looking at its key concepts and principles. This will be followed by details of the procedures under the HRA and, finally, by an examination of the main non-discrimination provision, Article 14.

SECTION 1

THE CONVENTION

The HRA incorporated most of the main provisions of the Convention into domestic law. This means that individuals can now rely on those rights in UK courts and tribunals. The incorporated Convention rights are set out in the Appendix, together with the text of the HRA. Subsequent chapters will explore how those rights can be used to tackle racial discrimination and racist behaviour in various walks of life.

The Council of Europe
The Convention is a treaty of the Council of Europe. The Council of Europe is a European intergovernmental organisation established after the Second World War with responsibilities for the promotion of democracy, human rights and the rule of law throughout the member states in Europe. It is based in Strasbourg. The Convention was adopted in 1950 and was ratified by the UK in 1951.

The European Court of Human Rights
The European Court of Human Rights (ECtHR) is better known than the Council of Europe. It is the judicial body of the Council of Europe and has jurisdiction for the supervision and interpretation of the Convention. The

European Commission of Human Rights (ECommHR) used to decide on the admissibility of applications to the ECtHR, and provided an opinion on the merits of any particular application. It was abolished in November 1998.

What is often referred to as 'Strasbourg case law' therefore includes both the judgments of the ECtHR and the decisions of the ECommHR.

In order to understand how to interpret the Convention it is necessary to become familiar with some of its key concepts, principles and language. These are:

- The hierarchy of rights;
- The concept of 'necessary in a democratic society';
- 'Proportionality';
- The 'margin of appreciation';
- 'Purposive' interpretation.

The purpose of this section is to provide a summary only of these often overlapping concepts and principles. Strasbourg case law further defines and interprets these concepts but it is outside the scope of this book to present those arguments here. Lay advisers should note that there are complex issues of interpretation and that legal advice will often be necessary.

The hierarchy of rights

There is a hierarchy of Convention rights and questions of their interpretation and breach will depend on whether they are absolute, limited or qualified.

Absolute rights

A right is said to be absolute when there can be no derogation in peacetime and no justification in any circumstances for breach. Absolute rights include Article 3 (prohibition of torture) and Article 4(1) (prohibition of slavery).

Limited rights

Many Convention rights can be limited in circumstances defined by the Convention. Limited rights include Article 2 (right to life), Article 4(2) (prohibition of compulsory or forced labour), Article 5 (right to liberty and security), Article 6 (right to a fair trial), Article 7 (no punishment without law), Article 12 (right to marry), Article 14 (prohibition of discrimination), and Articles 1, 2 and 3 of Protocol 1 (respectively protection of property, right to education and right to free elections).

An example of a limitation is given in Article 5. This provides that everyone has the right to liberty and security of person and that no one shall be deprived of his liberty save in the circumstances specified within Article 5 and in accordance with a procedure prescribed by law. The set of circumstances set out in Article 5 includes detention for the interrogation of a suspect during a criminal investigation or for persons of unsound mind. Detention on these grounds is lawful, but it must accord with legal procedures.

Qualified rights

Qualified rights permit restrictions in the enjoyment of the right but there must be justification for the restriction. The justification must be based in law, necessary in a democratic society (see below), and must relate to one of the aims set out in the relevant article (such as the prevention of crime or the protection of public order or health).

Qualified rights include Article 8 (right to respect for private and family life), Article 9 (freedom of thought, conscience and religion), Article 10 (freedom of expression) and Article 11 (freedom of assembly and association).

An example of a restriction is given in Article 8. Article 8(1) provides that everyone has the right to respect for his private and family life, his home and his correspondence. Article 8(2) provides that there shall be no interference by a public authority with the exercise of this right except such as is in accordance with the law and is necessary in a democratic society in the interests of national security, public safety or the economic well-being of the country, for the prevention of disorder or crime, for the protection of health or morals, or for the protection of the rights and freedoms of others.

The treatment of prisoners' correspondence is an example of a restriction to Article 8. Strasbourg case law has established that it is justifiable (in order to prevent crime) for prison authorities to interfere with prisoners' correspondence if it contains threats of violence or discussion of crime and disorder. Legal correspondence, by contrast, is privileged and should not be read.

Necessary in a democratic society

A restriction on a qualified right may be permitted where it is 'necessary in a democratic society'. This means that the restriction must fulfil a pressing social need, pursue a legitimate aim, and that there must be a reasonable relationship of proportionality between the means employed and the aim pursued. The concept of proportionality is explained further below.

Proportionality

The principle of proportionality is a central theme in human rights law. In simple terms, it means that, where a public authority decides to adopt a particular measure that interferes with the enjoyment of a limited or qualified right, the measure must be strictly proportionate to the legitimate aim it pursues. This is sometimes referred to as the 'fair balance test'; in practice, it often requires a balancing exercise between the rights of the individual and the public interest.

Until the HRA came into force, public authorities had to consider whether their policies or acts were lawful by reference to case law on judicial review. This set out standards for assessing the reasonableness or rationality of such policies or acts, which were often difficult to overcome. Further analysis of judicial review principles is contained in the chapter on social welfare. To satisfy the test for proportionality, however, a public authority will have to go further. It must now ask whether its policies or acts:

• Interfere with the enjoyment of a Convention right;
• Have objectives that are legitimate or sufficiently important;
• Have any alternative that could achieve the same objectives with little or no impairment of the enjoyment of a Convention right; and
• Might be formulated to impair as little as possible the enjoyment of Convention rights.

Importantly, even if public authorities are able to satisfy the proportionality test, the policies or acts adopted may still not be justified if their interference with Convention rights is too severe.

One example can be given by reference by Article 9. In a multi-faith society, it may be necessary to place restrictions on Article 9 – the manifestation of religious beliefs – to protect those who do not want to be subjected to a vigorous campaign to convert or recruit members. However, a general prohibition on such activities would be disproportionately wide.

Margin of appreciation

The 'margin of appreciation' is a fundamental doctrine of Convention law. It is an acknowledgement by the ECtHR that, in relation to issues such as national security, morality and social and economic policy, the national authorities (courts and government) are in a better position to make a decision on the compatibility of policy or law with the Convention. Accordingly, the ECtHR will allow national decision-makers a fair amount of latitude in how they apply the Convention.

It has been argued that it is inappropriate for national courts and tribunals to apply the doctrine of the margin of appreciation in the same way as ECtHR. This is because the ECtHR is an international court that recognises the differences in the customs and norms of each State. The same cannot be said of national courts and tribunals, which are familiar with national customs and therefore competent to make decisions on compatibility. However, it is likely that decision-makers will have some discretion in how they apply the Convention, most likely in areas of political, social and economic policy and particularly where there are resource implications.

Purposive interpretation

The Convention is a living instrument intended to respond to modern conditions. It is therefore often given a 'purposive' interpretation; this means that the courts will look at the object and purpose of the law and give a practical and effective interpretation to Convention rights. Readers will be familiar with the efforts that the courts have on occasion made to give domestic anti-discrimination law a 'purposive' interpretation. The same applies to human rights principles and, consequently, strict principles of statutory construction will often not apply to the interpretation of the Convention.

SECTION 2

THE HRA

As previously mentioned, the impact of the HRA will be far reaching. But, to be able to know how and when to use the HRA, advisers will need to know·

- Who is bound by the HRA;
- Which activities are caught;
- Who can be a victim;
- Procedures for complaints; and
- Remedies.

Who is bound by the HRA?

Public authorities

The HRA is binding on all public authorities. Public authorities must act compatibly with the Convention and can be held accountable in the courts if they do not.

The HRA does not provide a definition of 'public authority', but the scheme of the HRA provides for three broad categories of public authority. It is important to understand these categories as, in some of the later sections, such as employment law, they will determine whether a victim can actually commence court or tribunal proceedings under the HRA.

1. *'Pure' Public Authorities*
These include central and local government and other manifestly obvious public bodies, such as the Immigration and Nationality Directorate, the Department of Social Security, the Child Support Agency, health authorities and NHS trusts, police authorities and police forces, and the prison service.

2. *'Hybrid' Public Authorities*
These include any person or organisation carrying out certain functions of a public nature. These will usually be private bodies, but they will be considered as a public authority in relation to their public functions and not their private acts. Examples include the utilities' boards, Railtrack and providers of services contracted out by central and local government.

3. *Courts And Tribunals*
The distinction between pure and hybrid public authorities raises complex issues in terms of defining 'functions of a public nature' and private acts. In particular, it appears from the wording of s.6 HRA that hybrid public authorities are under no duty to comply with Convention rights when carrying out private acts (e.g. the purchase of land) but pure public authorities are under a duty to comply with Convention rights in *everything* that they do. There are no clear answers to this but it is important for advisers to recognise the problems and to seek legal advice where appropriate.

Private persons

The application of the Convention to private individuals is sometimes referred to as 'horizontal effect'.

The HRA is not binding on private individuals (unless they perform functions of a public nature) and so as a general rule cannot be relied upon in private disputes. This is because human rights law is primarily concerned with the relationship between the individual and the state. However, there are limited circumstances when it may be possible to rely on the HRA in private disputes. This is most likely to arise in cases where there is a gap in legislation for which the Government is held accountable. Individual examples are given in the forthcoming chapters.

It may also be possible to apply the HRA in private disputes where there are proceedings before a court or tribunal. This is because, as stated above, courts and tribunals are themselves public authorities and so are bound to comply with Convention rights. This means that they will have to interpret legislation and the common law in accordance with Convention rights even in cases where the dispute is between private persons.

The application of the HRA in private disputes is a complex area and it is again recommended that legal advice be sought where appropriate.

Which activities are caught?

Public authorities are not only under a duty to refrain from interfering with Convention rights; in certain circumstances, they must take positive measures to secure and protect Convention rights. This means that public authorities can be held accountable not only for acts and decisions but also for their omissions and failures to act.

One example relates to the alleged failure by the police to act on repeated complaints by a person of racial harassment and assault, which result in the death of that person. This may amount to a breach of the Article 2 right to life, as public authorities are under a limited obligation to preserve life.

Who can be a victim?

A person can bring a claim under the HRA only if he or she is or is likely to be a victim of a breach of a Convention right. There are therefore two circumstances in which a person can be a victim: where he or she is directly affected by an act, decision or omission which breaches a Convention right; or where he or she runs the risk of being directly affected.

A victim can be:

- An individual;
- Relatives of a deceased victim where the complaint is about the victim's death;
- A company;
- A trade union; or
- A non-governmental organisation or group of individuals.

It is important to appreciate, however counter-intuitive it may seem, that the HRA may be used by companies, which are legal entities in their own right. This may raise some interesting and controversial issues, particularly where there are competing rights between companies and individuals, such as between developers and communities. NGOs and organisations like trades unions can only bring cases in their own name if they are (or are likely to be) directly affected. They cannot bring proceedings in their own name to protect the rights of their members – although of course they will be able to fund proceedings brought by their members.

Procedure for complaints

There are two routes for bringing proceedings against a public authority. These are set out in s.7 HRA. A victim may take a public authority directly to court or tribunal for breaching his/her right; or may rely on the Convention right or rights concerned in the course of other proceedings (such as criminal proceedings, employment tribunal proceedings, judicial review, immigration or Social Security tribunal proceedings). Further details are given in the subsequent chapters.

Limitation period

Where a victim takes a public authority directly to court then the limitation period in which to bring proceedings is *one year* beginning with the date on which the act complained of took place. The courts have a discretion to extend this period where they consider it 'equitable having regard to all the circumstances'. It is essential to note the existence of this limitation period, as it will not be referred to in all of the subsequent chapters.

This limitation period only applies where the public authority is taken directly to court for breach of a Convention right. Advisers should take note that a stricter time limit may be imposed where the victim relies on a Convention right in other proceedings. Examples are given in subsequent chapters of stricter time limits that may shorten this one-year period. Legal advice should always be sought on limitation matters where appropriate.

Retrospective effect

The HRA does not apply to acts done by a public authority *before* the date of implementation (i.e. before 2 October 2000). However, a victim will be able to rely on the Convention in relation to acts or omission made before the date of implementation where the proceedings were brought by a public authority, and the proceedings are pending at the date of implementation.

Remedies

Where a court or tribunal finds that a public authority has breached a Convention right, it may grant such relief or remedy or make such order within its powers as it considers 'just and appropriate'.

The remedy will not always be damages; the nature of the remedy will vary depending on the facts of the case. For example, in criminal proceedings, the remedy might be the exclusion of evidence or the quashing of a conviction. In judicial review proceedings, the remedy might be the quashing of a decision. In other cases, it might be the award of damages. In all cases, the remedy must be 'just and appropriate' and effective.

There are some limitations to the power to award damages. First, damages may only be awarded by a court or tribunal with similar power to award damages in civil proceedings. Secondly, no award of damages is to be made unless, taking account of all the circumstances of the case, the court is satisfied that the award is necessary to afford just satisfaction to the victim.

When awarding damages, courts must also take into account the principles applied by the ECtHR. The awards of ECtHR are based on the principle of 'just satisfaction' and it is important to note that this has tended in the past to yield only modest amounts by way of damages.

SECTION 3

PARLIAMENT AND THE COURTS

The HRA has resulted in significant constitutional reform of the legislature, executive and judiciary.

Legislature
The HRA requires the Government to certify that future legislation is compatible with Convention rights. If the Government cannot so certify then Ministers must give reasons for non-compatibility when presenting draft legislation before Parliament.

Executive
This has implications for the Executive, which must carry out human rights assessments of proposed legislation and policy before Ministers can make the above statement of compatibility.

Judiciary
Under the scheme of the HRA, the courts assume an important role in protecting rights and developing a human rights culture. In particular, the courts' role is as follows:

- As public authorities, to interpret the statutory and common law in a manner compatible with the Convention, even in private disputes, and so permit limited horizontal application of the Convention;
- To make declarations of incompatibility. The High Court, the Court of Appeal and the House of Lords all have the power to declare that *primary* legislation (i.e. Acts of Parliament) is incompatible with the Convention. Primary legislation cannot be struck down. However, all courts have the power to disregard incompatible *secondary* legislation (e.g. statutory instruments); and
- To develop a human rights case law for the UK. The HRA obliges the courts to have regard to Strasbourg case law – but there is no duty to follow it. The Strasbourg case law provides the minimum standard below which the case law of the UK courts should not fall; in other words, it sets a floor, not a ceiling, of rights.

When interpreting the Convention the courts may refer to other international human rights treaties (which often provide greater protection than the Convention) such as the European Social Charter, the International Covenant on Civil and Political Rights, the Convention on the Rights of the Child, the International Convention on the Elimination of all Forms of Racial Discrimination and the International Convention on the Elimination of Discrimination Against Women. The courts may also refer to the judgments of foreign courts e.g. the Supreme Courts of Canada, South Africa and India. These additional sources of law will often prove helpful.

SECTION 4

DISCRIMINATION AND THE CONVENTION

The avoidance of irrational discrimination is a central theme in human rights law. All human rights treaties provide in one form or another that rights should be enjoyed without discrimination on various prohibited grounds. However, there is very little Strasbourg case law on racial discrimination; this is due in part to the limited scope of the non-discrimination provision in the Convention (Article 14) and also to the approach taken by the ECtHR to its application.

Article 14 declares that: 'The enjoyment of the rights and freedoms set forth in this Convention shall be enjoyed without discrimination on any ground such as sex, race, colour, language, religion, political or other opinion, national or social origin, association with a minority, property, birth or other status.' There are a number of observations to make about Article 14.

Prohibited forms of discrimination
A positive feature of Article 14 is the non-exhaustive list of prohibited grounds. Plainly it includes the most common grounds such as sex, race, colour and religion. But inclusion of the words 'grounds such as' and 'or other status' show clearly that the list of grounds is evolutionary. For example, it is now widely accepted that Article 14 covers disability, age and sexual orientation, even though it explicitly mentions none of these.

In principle, this makes Article 14 sufficiently broad to respond to new and developing issues of inequality. It is likely that the UK courts will be asked to apply Article 14 to further grounds beyond those it specifically lists, but it remains to be seen how broad an approach the courts will adopt.

Reasonable and objective justification
Not every discrimination or difference in treatment will be regarded as

unlawful discrimination under Article 14. The ECtHR has held that discrimination may be lawful where:

* There is a reasonable and objective justification; and
* It is seen to pursue a legitimate aim; and
* There is a reasonable relationship of proportionality between the means employed and the aim sought.

These concepts were introduced above. The burden of proof in any particular case lies on the responding public authority to establish that there is a legitimate aim for the difference in treatment. If the public authority succeeds in showing a legitimate aim, then the burden of proof passes to the victim to show a lack of proportionality. The standard of the burden of proof on the victim can vary according to the ground of discrimination.

The defence of justification is not new to domestic practitioners of anti-discrimination law: justification is a defence to indirect (but not direct) discrimination under the RRA (see subsequent chapters). However, under Strasbourg case law, objective justification is a defence to both indirect *and direct* discrimination.

Given that the RR(A)A will extend the prohibition of direct and indirect discrimination to all public authorities that are similarly bound by the Convention, the defence of objective justification would appear to be at odds with the RRA in relation to direct discrimination. It is not yet clear how the courts will approach this discrepancy: it has been argued that Strasbourg case law provides the *minimum* standard of protection and where the national law provides a higher standard then the courts should not depart from that higher standard; it is equally open to Respondents to argue that the denial of the defence of objective justification to direct discrimination may breach their Article 6 right to a fair trial, in particular the right to equality of arms and to participate effectively in the proceedings. However, restrictions can be placed on the enjoyment of Article 6 rights provided the aim of the restriction is legitimate and proportionate. It will ultimately be for the courts to determine whether or not the absence of a defence of justification to direct discrimination under the RRA is itself compatible with the Convention

Suspect classes
Strasbourg case law shows that some grounds of discrimination carry a higher level of protection; these grounds are referred to as 'suspect grounds' or 'suspect classes'. The grounds of race and sex, for example, are suspect classes. They developed as 'suspect classes' because their impact on society is more obvious than, say, discrimination on grounds of corpo-

rate status. With 'suspect classes', a higher level of scrutiny has been used by the ECtHR to determine whether a discriminatory measure satisfies the above criteria and is consequently lawful. Where the ground of discrimination is considered to be 'suspect', the burden on the victim to show lack of proportionality will be low.

Affirmative action
The defence of objective justification may be used creatively to allow for affirmative action measures: these are likely to be lawful and a defence to direct discrimination provided they can be reasonably and objectively justified.

Scope of Article 14
Disappointingly, Article 14 does not guarantee a freestanding right to equality and freedom from discrimination. There is no mention of a right to equality and the prohibition on discrimination applies to the enjoyment of other Convention rights only. It means that Article 14 can only be used in conjunction with a Convention right. Indeed, it is often referred to as 'parasitic' on account of its accessory or dependent nature. Importantly, it is not necessary to show a *breach* of that other Convention right in order to activate Article 14; merely that the claim in issue falls within the ambit of another Convention right. This is a common theme throughout this book.

Additional Protocol 12
By comparison, Article 26 ICCPR contains a stronger provision. It provides that: 'All persons are equal before the law and are entitled without any discrimination to the equal protection of the law. In this respect, the law shall prohibit any discrimination and guarantee to all persons equal and effective protection against discrimination on any ground such as race, colour, sex, language, religion, political or other opinion, national or social origin, property, birth or other status.'

The difference between the two treaties illustrates the age and imperfections of the Convention. However, in Spring 2000, the Council of Europe approved a protocol to strengthen Article 14 of the Convention. Additional Protocol 12 provides that:

1. The enjoyment of any right set forth by law shall be secured without discrimination on any ground such as sex, race, colour, language, religion, political or other opinion, national or social origin, association with a national minority, property, birth or other status.
2. No-one shall be discriminated against by a public authority on any ground such as those mentioned in paragraph 1.

Additional Protocol 12 opened for signature on 4 November 2000 and required ten Member States to sign and ratify it before it could come into force in any of their countries. Any Member State who has not signed and ratified it will not be bound by it.

The HRA did not incorporate Additional Protocol 12 and nor did the UK Government separately ratify it. At the time of publication, the position of the UK Government is that it has no present plans to ratify it.

SECTION 5

SOME KEY CONVENTION CASES

Although this is not designed to be a legal textbook, readers may wish to know the names of key Convention cases. Some of them are below.

Race & Discrimination

Objective and reasonable justification
Belgian Linguistics Case (No 1) [1968] 1 EHRR 252

Other prohibited grounds
Sutherland v UK [1998] EHRLR, *Affaire Salgueiro da Silva Mouta v Portugal*
    [Case No. 33290/96] – sexual orientation
Marckxz v Belgium [1979] 2 EHRR 330 – illegitimacy
Rasmussen v Denmark [1984] 7 EHRR 371 – marital status
Buckley v UK [1996] 23 EHRR 101 – gypsies

Suspect groups
Abdulaziz, Cabales and Balkandali v UK [1985] 7 EHRR 471
East African Asians v UK [1973] 3 EHRR 76

Racism as inhuman and degrading treatment
East African Asians v UK [1973] 3 EHRR 76

Race hatred
Glimmerveen and Hagenbeek v Netherlands [1979] 18 DR 187 – reliance on
    article 17 to justify prosecution of the applicants for possessing leaflets
    likely to incite racial hatred and their exclusion from local elections

Proportionality
Malone v UK A/82 [1984] 7 EHRR 14 & *Halford v UK* [1997] 24 EHRR 523

– there must be some basis in national law for a restriction and national law must be accessible and precise.

Soering v UK [1989] 11 EHRR 439 – court's observations on the need for a fair balance between the rights of the individual and the interests of the wider community.

Purposive interpretation

Cossey v UK 24 [1990] 13 EHRR 622 – the Convention must be interpreted as a 'living instrument' in light of present-day conditions

Tyrer v UK [1978] 2 EHRR 1

Other

Airey v Ireland [1979] 2 EHRR 305 – effective right of access to a court of full jurisdiction (which must include free legal aid in the interests of justice in criminal cases and may include it in complex civil matters).

The Race Relations Act and other legislation to combat racism and racial discrimination

Barbara Cohen

The focus of this book is how the HRA can provide new scope to challenge racial discrimination. However, in deciding how best to use the law, it remains important to consider *all* the legislation that offers the possibility of redress for racist behaviour or racial discrimination. This chapter provides an overview of that legislative framework.

The main legislation in this context is obviously the RRA. The RR(A)A extends the scope of the RRA and imposes an enforceable race equality duty on all of the main public authorities. Further amendments of the RRA will be required by July 2003 under the terms of the EC Race Directive. The criminal law also offers some protection against racist behaviour, including the offences in the POA concerned with incitement of racial hatred and the racially aggravated offences in the CDA. Other criminal statutes can be used in relation to racist behaviour and local authorities and other bodies can use their powers to prevent or impose sanctions on racially discriminatory behaviour.

RRA

The RRA makes it unlawful to discriminate (directly, indirectly or by victim- isation) in certain types of activities. It is concerned with discrimination on racial grounds. This covers discrimination on grounds of race, colour, nationality (including citizenship), ethnic origin and national origin. Most cases under the RRA relate to the race or colour of the victim, but the RRA also prevents discrimination where the 'racial grounds' refer to the race of other persons. One example is where white persons are refused admittance to a club because their group includes black friends. Another example is where an employee is dismissed because he or she refused to carry out racially discriminatory instructions.

The RRA offers civil law remedies. The fact that certain acts are defined as unlawful discrimination makes it possible for individuals who are victims of such discrimination to bring proceedings and, if successful, to be awarded compensation. The main way that unlawful racial discrimination can be challenged is by individual victims complaining to a court or tribunal. The RRA established the Commission for Racial Equality, which has special powers to challenge and stop discriminatory practices.

Defining discrimination
There are three types of unlawful discrimination under the RRA: direct discrimination, indirect discrimination and victimisation. It is important to understand these properly as reference to them is made throughout this book.

Direct discrimination
This simply means less favourable treatment on racial grounds. Direct discrimination can be shown where it is obvious that the treatment is on racial grounds (such as racial harassment). It can also be shown where there is evidence that a person of a different racial group (known as the 'comparator') would not in the same or similar circumstances have received the same treatment. The RRA specifies that segregation by racial group is less favourable treatment.

Indirect discrimination
This is perhaps the most difficult concept in the RRA. It is concerned with the imposition of a condition or requirement – not necessarily formally adopted but operating within an organisation – that is not in itself discrim-inatory, but in its application it operates to the disadvantage of a particular racial group where members of that group are proportionately less able to comply with it.

Another way of putting it is that, while direct discrimination involves application of a racially specific criterion ('no blacks need apply'), indirect discrimination involves the application of an apparently racially neutral criterion that may nonetheless have a disparate impact on a particular racial group. Examples include a language requirement for a job and giving priority on a popular council housing estate to sons and daughters of tenants on that estate. Indirect discrimination is unlawful unless it can be justified on non-racial grounds.

Victimisation
This means treating a person less favourably than other persons because the person has complained of discrimination. This includes bringing

proceedings personally and supporting proceedings brought by another person. However, it will not be victimisation if the allegation of discrimination was false and not made in good faith.

Activities to which the RRA applies

The RRA does not offer a universal ban on all racial discrimination. Its scope is defined to include only certain types of activities that, loosely, are those where there is some degree of formality in the relationship between the parties. The main areas in which the RRA prohibits discrimination include:

- Employment (which is defined to include apprenticeship and a contract with a person who is self-employed);
- Conferring qualifications for a trade or profession;
- Vocational training;
- Membership of trade union or employers' or professional associations;
- Partnerships (currently those with 6 or more partners);
- Education;
- Housing;
- Planning control;
- Provision of goods, facilities or services; and
- Membership of clubs and associations.

The RR(A)A has added further areas in which discrimination is outlawed:

- Carrying out further public functions, such as policing, running prisons, running detention centres, collecting taxes, detaining mental patients, local authority enforcement, immigration control (with some exceptions) and customs and excise;
- Holding public office.

In each of these areas it is unlawful to discriminate directly, indirectly or by way of victimisation. It is not necessary to prove that the discriminator *intended* to discriminate, merely that one of the above forms of discrimination occurred.

The Employment Tribunal hears complaints of racial discrimination relating to employment. A tribunal must receive an application no later than three months less one day from the act of discrimination forming the basis of the complaint. Legal advice should always be sought on time limits.

Complaints of discrimination in other areas are made to the County Court; the time limit to begin County Court proceedings is six months less one day from the act of discrimination. However, the civil procedure rules generally require a letter setting out the complaint in detail to have been sent to the alleged discriminator before court proceedings are begun.

The person who brings a complaint of racial discrimination is expected to prove their case on a balance of probabilities. This can be very difficult, since victims of discrimination know they have been treated unfairly but it is often only the discriminator who will know why. Under the present law, where a court or tribunal finds that there has been a difference in treatment and a difference in race, and if the alleged discriminator fails to offer an adequate or satisfactory explanation for the difference in treatment, then the court or tribunal may – but are not required to – draw an inference of racial discrimination and uphold the complaint. Many cases are finely balanced and the outcome often depends on the willingness of the court or tribunal to draw such an inference.

If a complaint of discrimination is upheld, the court or tribunal can make a declaration to this effect and may award compensation. Compensation can relate both to the financial loss the victim has suffered (or will suffer) as a result of the discrimination and also to what is called 'injured feelings'. If there has been damage to the person's physical or (more often) mental health, the court may also award damages for personal injury.

Average awards in the Employment Tribunal are less than £10,000. However, where the victim of discrimination has had a high salary and loses both that salary and future pension entitlements, or where tribunals accept that the seriousness of the damage to mental health is such that the victim is unlikely to work again, compensation can be very substantial indeed (in exceptional cases in six figures). Awards in the County Court rarely exceed £1,000.

The RRA also makes it unlawful to publish an advertisement indicating an intention to discriminate or to instruct another person or to induce or attempt to induce another person to commit an act of unlawful discrimination.

The CRE has powers to assist individuals who wish to bring proceedings for racial discrimination. The CRE can conduct formal investigations and issue non-discrimination notices where an investigation exposes acts of unlawful discrimination. The CRE can bring proceedings for discriminatory advertisements or pressure or instructions to discriminate and can apply for injunctions to stop persistent discrimination.

RR(A)A

As stated above, the RR(A)A has extended the scope of the RRA so that it is unlawful for any public authority to discriminate directly, indirectly, or by victimisation in the carrying out of any of its functions. A public authority is, for this purpose, defined in the same way as a public authority under the HRA (see the Introduction, above), but excludes judicial acts and legislative functions of Parliament. It therefore includes organisations that are carrying out functions of a public nature, for example, private companies managing prisons or immigration detention centres.

One significant exception is that discrimination on grounds of nationality or ethnic or national origin (but not race or colour) will *not* be unlawful in carrying out certain immigration and nationality functions where the discrimination is authorised under statute or the Immigration Rules or by a government minister.

The other significant change under the RR(A)A is the imposition of a statutory duty which requires specified public authorities in the carrying out of their functions to have due regard to the need to eliminate unlawful racial discrimination and to promote equality of opportunity and good race relations. Under an order by the Home Secretary, most major public authorities are required to publish a race equality scheme setting out how they will carry out certain processes, including consultation on new policies and monitoring their current policies for adverse impact on race equality. The CRE has issued a code of practice giving practical guidance, which can be referred to in legal proceedings. Where a public authority fails to comply with the Home Secretary's order, they can be required to do so through a compliance notice served by the CRE and ultimately enforced by the County Court.

European Race Directive

In June 2000, the EU Council of Ministers unanimously approved a new directive implementing the principle of equal treatment between persons irrespective of racial or ethnic origin. The Directive requires all Member States to take steps by July 2003 to ensure that their national legislation is consistent with the Directive. It sets common minimum standards. It prohibits member states from reducing any protection existing in their legislation that is of a higher standard.

While the UK has better developed anti-discrimination legislation than many others EU member states, the Directive will require significant amendment to the RRA. To this end, in October 2002, the DTI issued for consultation the draft Race Relations Act 1976 (Amendment) Regulations 2003. The main areas where there will need to be amendments are:

- The definition of indirect discrimination: the new definition will need to be wider and more inclusive than the existing one;
- The burden of proof: this will need to be changed so that when the victim of discrimination establishes facts from which it may be presumed that there has been direct or indirect discrimination, the

alleged discriminator will need to prove that there has not been unlawful discrimination;

- Racial harassment will be defined specifically as a form of unlawful discrimination;
- Exceptions: fewer exceptions of unlawful discrimination will be permitted, with more rigorous requirements to justify any exceptions;
- Sanctions awarded by courts and tribunals: these will have to be strengthened; and
- Laws and regulations conflicting with the principle of equal recruitment irrespective of racial or ethnic origin: any such laws or regulations will need to be abolished.

CRIMINAL OFFENCES

The criminal law increasingly recognises the harm that racism and racist behaviour can do, and there are now a number of criminal offences specifically intended to prevent and to punish racist behaviour. Any suspected offence should be reported to the police without delay. Prosecution is normally by the CPS. The burden of proof is stricter: a person should be convicted only if the magistrates or the jury are satisfied of their guilt beyond reasonable doubt, not on a balance of probabilities.

Inciting racial hatred
The first RRA in 1965 introduced a criminal offence of incitement of racial hatred. Similar offences were in the 1968 and 1976 RRA. Now Part III POA includes six separate offences relating to the incitement of racial hatred.

For all these offences, the key elements are words or behaviour or material in any form that is threatening, abusive or insulting and that, by their actions, the person intends to stir up racial hatred or in all the circumstances racial hatred is likely to be stirred up. Racial hatred is defined as hatred against a group of persons in Great Britain defined by reference to colour, race, nationality (including citizenship) or ethnic or national origins.

The offences in Part III POA include:

- s.18: using words or behaviour or displaying written material;
- s.19: publishing or distributing written material;
- s.20: presenting or directing the public performance;
- s.21: distributing, showing or playing a film, video, sound recording etc;
- s.22: broadcasting a programme including abusive or insulting images or sound; the offence is committed by any persons involved in providing

the service or producing or directing the programme or using the words or behaviour; and
- s.23: possessing written material or film, video or sound recording which is threatening, abusive, or insulting or a recording with a view to displaying, publishing or distributing or broadcasting the material.

Proceedings for any of the above offences require the consent of the Attorney General. In practice, relatively few cases each year are brought. It would seem that this is not as result of refusal by the Attorney General but because the CPS refers only a handful of cases.

A person convicted for any of the above offences in the crown court can be sentenced to up to two years' imprisonment or a fine or both, and on conviction in the magistrates' court imprisonment for up to six months or a fine or both.

FOA

S.3 FOA makes it an offence to engage or take part in chanting of 'a racialist nature' at an association football match. In this context, 'chanting' means the repeated uttering of any words or sounds (whether alone or with others), and 'of a racialist nature' means consisting of or including matter which is threatening, abusive, or insulting to a person by reason of his colour, race, nationality (including citizenship) or ethnic or national origins. The offence can be committed during the period beginning two hours before the match is advertised to start and one hour after the end of the match. An offence under the FOA is punishable by a fine not exceeding £1,000.

CDA

Racially aggravated offences
With a view to demonstrating the seriousness with which racist crime is regarded, the Government introduced in the CDA nine new racially aggravated offences. In each the element of racial aggravation has been incorporated into existing offences, with the racially aggravated form of the offence attracting a more severe sentence.

The CDA offers two alternative tests for racial aggravation:

1. At the time of committing the offence, or immediately before or after doing so, the offender demonstrates towards the victim hostility based on the victim's membership (or presumed membership) of a racial group; or
2. The offence is motivated (wholly or partly) by hostility towards members of a racial group based on their membership of that group.

'Racial group' is defined as in the RRA (see above), and 'membership' includes association with members of a group, so a white person known to have close friends who are black could be the victim of a racially aggravated offence.

The offences that can be racially aggravated are:

- Malicious wounding or grievous bodily harm (s.20 OPA);
- Actual bodily harm (s.45 OPA);
- Common assault;
- Criminal damage (s.1 CrimDA);
- Abusive or insulting words or behaviour intending to cause unlawful violence or to provoke unlawful violence (s.4 POA);
- Using threatening abusive or insulting words or disorderly behaviour with intent to cause a person harassment, alarm or distress (s.4(a) POA);
- Using abusive insulting words or behaviour of disorderly behaviour, displaying any written signs etc within the sight or hearing of a person likely to be caused harassment, alarm or distress (s.5 POA);
- Conduct on at least two occasions which amounts to harassment of another person (s.2 PHA); and
- Conduct on at least two occasions that causes another person to fear that violence will be used against them (s.4 PHA).

Following conviction of offences under the PHA above, and in order to protect the victim from further harassment or fear of violence, the court may impose a restraining order prohibiting the defendant from doing specified acts. Breach of a restraining order is an offence, punishable by imprisonment for up to five years.

In addition to the specific racially aggravated offences listed above, s.82 CDA imposes a duty on a court sentencing for any other offence that is racially aggravated to treat that fact as a factor that increases the seriousness of the offence.

Antisocial behaviour orders

Under the CDA, either a local authority or the police, each acting in consultation with the other, can apply to the magistrates' court for an antisocial behaviour order. The court will need to be satisfied that the particular individuals aged 10 or over have caused harassment, alarm or distress to one or more other persons and that an order is necessary to protect persons in the area from further antisocial acts by these individuals. An order prohibits the persons from doing specified acts and will have effect for a minimum period of 2 years; breach of the order is a criminal offence punishable by imprisonment by up to 5 years or a fine, or both. Antisocial behaviour orders could be used where particular individuals can be identified as persistently causing racial harassment in a local area.

This process has been criticised because quite draconian orders can be issued on the civil standard of proof. Further, as local authorities and the police are expected to have attempted other steps to control harassment, with applying to the court as a last resort, relatively few antisocial behaviour orders have been made. Some amendments are expected in the Police Reform Bill 2002.

MCA

Race-hate mail could be prosecuted under the MCA. S.1 MCA makes it an offence to send to another person a letter or other article which conveys a message which is grossly offensive or a threat, or information which is false and known to be false by the sender, or any article which is in whole or in part of a grossly offensive nature, if the purpose of sending such item is that is likely to cause distress or anxiety to the recipient or any other person whom it is intended should see or be told about what has been sent.

The maximum sentence is a fine of £2,500.

TA

Under s.43 TA, it is an offence for a person to send by telephone a message or other matter that is grossly offensive or indecent, obscene or menacing in character, or send by telephone for the purpose of causing annoyance, inconvenience or needless anxiety to another a message that he knows to be false, or persistently makes use for that purpose of the telephone system. This offence was used to convict a BNP caller who made repeat calls of a grossly offensive racist nature to an Asian man.

The offence carries a six-month sentence.

The limitation of both of these offences is that they can, of course, be applied only where the sender or the caller can be identified.

Some local authority powers to tackle racial harassment

Under s.144 HA, a local authority can apply to the court for an order enabling them to evict a tenant where the tenant or a person living or visiting the tenant's home has been guilty of conduct causing or likely to cause a nuisance or annoyance to any persons residing, visiting or otherwise lawfully present in the area. The same grounds are available for private sector landlord in relation to assured tenancies.

Under s.152 HA, a local authority may apply to the court for an injunction to prohibit a person from engaging in or threatening to engage in conduct causing or likely to cause nuisance or annoyance to persons residing in or visiting or otherwise lawfully present in local authority house or flat. The court will only grant an injunction if it is satisfied that the respondent has used or threatened to use violence against any such persons and there is a significant risk of harm to that person or persons of similar description if the injunction is not granted.

Under s.1 PFEA, it an offence to evict someone unlawfully from residential premises. It is also an offence for any person with intent to cause a person to give up all or part of residential premises to do any act that interferes with the peace or comfort of the occupier of the house or flat.

Normally the local authority will initiate prosecution for harassment and unlawful eviction. The maximum sentence for such offence is imprisonment for up to two years or a fine or both.

Criminal law and the rights of suspects

Sharon Persaud

This chapter examines the effect the HRA may have on the criminal justice system, and highlights areas where the rights of suspects, defendants and prisoners from the black or other minority communities may be in particular issue.

The chapter will look, in very broad terms, at the position of suspects and defendants as it was prior to the HRA coming into force, whether the HRA has created (and is creating) new rights and, lastly, where it may make a difference to the day-to-day experience of suspects and defendants.

The HRA has the potential to bolster the rights of the individual as against the state – in the criminal context, the rights of suspects and defendants as against the powers of the police and the judiciary – but it is likely to benefit defendants from ethnic minorities *as defendants*, rather than because of any particularly anti-discrimination agenda. Most of what follows therefore applies generally to suspects and defendants.

As advisers are most likely to be consulted at the police station or investigative stage, there is a particular focus on that area.

Advisers should also have regard to the recommendations set out in the Criminal Courts review by Lord Justice Auld, published in September 2001. If these recommendations are adopted, they may be susceptible to challenge in a number of areas.

SECTION 1

POSITION PRE-HRA

Overview of the criminal justice system
Prior to the HRA, individuals suspected of committing crimes or who were before the criminal courts had rights and entitlements – but these were

rarely expressed as positive rights. Instead, the system worked by limiting or prescribing the circumstances in which the state, in its various guises, could carry out its functions of investigation, or in bringing cases to trial.

The criminal law has to cover a lot of ground. It regulates police powers and procedure, court procedures, the grant of bail, the rules of evidence, powers of sentence – as well as, obviously, defining offences.

Because of its scope, the obligations of the state in dealing with individuals who are suspected of committing an offence are set out in many different places within 'the criminal law' – which makes giving detailed advice to someone who has been arrested or charged particularly difficult.

As an overview, however, the process runs as follows: investigation, arrest, detention, interview and charge by the police – though possibly after consultation with the CPS.

An individual then appears before a Magistrates Court, and decisions are taken on plea and venue – that is, whether a case will be heard in the Magistrates Court, or will be committed to the Crown Court. (The court also makes ancillary decisions on legal aid and bail.)

In either instance, a defendant will either plead guilty, in which case he will be sentenced, or not guilty, when his case will be listed for trial. If a case goes to trial, it is governed by various rules of evidence and procedure. If a defendant is to be sentenced, the general approach that the magistrate or judge should take is also set down.

Laws and rules regulate each of these stages, and events often experienced as arbitrary – like the grant or refusal of legal aid or bail, or the decision to bind someone over – should in fact have a traceable and rational basis. Often, it is only when that basis is identified that we can see whether the decision is susceptible to challenge.

Below, the rights of an individual at each stage of a typical set of criminal proceedings are examined. The discussion is weighted towards the investigative process, as that is when those rights are most under threat – and when people are least likely to be represented.

Suspects' general rights

In the main, prior to the HRA, suspects' rights were not positively expressed, and police powers were mainly regulated by PACE, and its five Codes of Practice (A to E), and the CJPOA, rather than by any notion of an individual's human rights.

Taking the second first, the CJPOA did away with the 'right to silence' by allowing a court to draw adverse inferences from a suspect's failure to answer questions in particular circumstances – and may well contain the provisions most susceptible to review under the HRA.

PACE has eleven parts, the most important of which deal with the following powers: stop and search, entry, search and seizure, arrest, detention, questioning and treatment (including taking samples). PACE also has key evidential provisions, including s.76 and s.78, which allow a court to exclude – i.e. not allow the prosecution to use – evidence, if it is obtained by oppression, is unreliable, or it would be 'adverse to the fairness of the proceedings' to do so. Even now that the HRA is in force, PACE is still the starting point for establishing a suspect's rights in relation to police powers.

In broad terms, the investigative powers in PACE operate on a 'reasonable suspicion' basis; for example, generally, the police have to have reasonable grounds to suspect that they will find a prohibited or stolen article before they can stop and search, and reasonable grounds to suspect that an arrestable offence has been committed – arrestable offences are defined within PACE – before they can arrest.

The other key police powers that PACE and the Codes regulate are: searches of premises and individuals, seizure of items, arrest, detention, the questioning of suspects – including in the taped interviews that will be before the court if they are charged, and to which the controversial 'adverse inference' attaches – the power to take intimate and non-intimate samples, and identification procedures. (Identification procedures are found in Code D, but are outside the remit of this chapter.)

In theory, suspects' rights on searches (Codes A and B) and arrest are formally protected by the 'reasonable grounds' test – which, if properly applied, should stop arbitrary harassment and detention.

Once someone is in detention, his or her rights are formally protected by Code C, and made real by the two most basic rights – not to be held *in communicado*, and to have free access to independent legal advice at any time.

Suspects' rights in the police station

Once suspects are detained, PACE and Code C lay down a detailed regime for their questioning and treatment which, like PACE as a whole, is designed to preserve a balance between the powers of the police to investigate crime and the 'rights' – though that word is not often used within PACE – of the suspect.

For example, PACE defines the role of a custody officer, specifies the conditions that have to be met for continuing detention, and builds in provisions for review by an independent officer. It also provides the framework for taking samples, fingerprints and photographs.

Code C spells out the vital basic rights – and here it does adopt the language of 'rights' – to have someone informed of arrest and to speak to an independent solicitor free of charge. Crucially, it also deals with the conditions of detention, the caution and special warnings under the CJPOA, interviews, interpreters, intimate and strip-searches, delay to the two basic rights, and vulnerable and mentally disordered suspects. (Advisers should note that the intimate search and sample provisions are particularly difficult.)

PACE is a compendious piece of legislation, which has been interpreted through hundreds of cases – and detailed consideration is outside the scope of this book. If a suspect is detained in a police station, he must be advised to obtain legal advice immediately – and, subject to s.58(6) PACE and Annex B to Code C, which lay down the circumstances in which access to advice can be delayed – he is entitled to that advice without delay. It is likely that once a solicitor is involved, a suspect's rights and entitlements will be more closely observed by the police.

Suspects' rights, searches and intrusive surveillance

Out of the context of an immediate crisis at the police station, advisers may be asked about the powers of the police to 'stop and search' individuals and vehicles, to search premises, and to carry out intrusive surveillance. Again, for most searches, PACE adopts a 'reasonable suspicion' test – or some variant of it.

A constable is permitted to stop and search if he has reasonable grounds for suspecting that he will find stolen or prohibited articles, or items for use in connection with certain specified offences. Code A, which deals with the statutory powers of stop and search, makes it clear that there must be some objective basis to the suspicion, and that personal factors like 'colour, age, hairstyle or dress' or 'stereotypes' cannot be enough.

Similarly, the police can search on a warrant – and PACE lays down the circumstances in which a warrant can be obtained – or where there are reasonable grounds to suspect that evidence relating to an arrestable offence is on the premises.

The position in relation to intrusive surveillance – that is, covert monitoring or recording – is rather different and, inevitably, rather complicated. In brief terms, the powers of the police and security services to carry out intrusive surveillance are set out in the SecSA, the ISA, the PA and, most importantly, RIPA.

Under the HRA, at least some of these provisions are likely to be incompatible with the Convention. A checklist of likely breaches is included below, as part of the overview of Article 5 issues. Again, however, these points are extremely technical, and if an individual seeks advice about their rights in this area, they should be advised to also seek specialist legal advice.

Suspect's rights and the decision to charge

Usually, the police take the decision on whether or not to charge a suspect with a criminal offence – and, in practical terms, there is little that a suspect can do about that decision, except to try to persuade the officer that there is insufficient evidence, or that a caution should be given, or that some other course is appropriate.

If the police seek the advice of the CPS or, in any case, after charge, when the file is passed to the CPS by the police, the CPS have a duty to review the prosecution to see that there is enough evidence – that is, if a conviction is more likely than not – and if it is in the public interest to proceed.

These two tests, and the factors to be taken into account are set out in the Code for Crown Prosecutors – which makes clear that a decision to prosecute should not be based on the prosecutor's view of the ethnic or national origin of the complainant, witness or defendant. If an offence is motivated by discrimination (because of race, sex, sexuality or religious and political beliefs), it is a 'public interest' factor in favour of prosecution.

At this stage, then, both suspects and complainants are entitled to make representations. The HRA now informs any public interest test, though the factual issues to be balanced have not changed dramatically. In certain limited circumstances, a decision to prosecute, or a decision not to prosecute, can be judicially reviewed.

A defendant's 'fair trial' rights

One of this chapter's themes has been the very empirical approach to rights in the criminal justice system. As we have seen, suspects and defendants already have various rights – but they are not expressed or experienced as that.

An obvious example is the legal aid scheme, which is in place to ensure that defendants who do not have enough money to instruct and pay a lawyer privately can secure representation. This is obviously part of a defendant's right to a fair trial – and a decision on the grant or refusal of legal aid can itself be reviewed. Often, however, legal aid is experienced as something administrative, in which a defendant can have little say – which is partly because, until now, the 'rights' element has not been highlighted.

Similarly, when a defendant is before the court, the requirement that he have a fair trial is safeguarded in a number of ways – although that purpose, and the legal framework behind it, is often obscured by the procedure and language of the courts.

In the magistrates' court, for example – and very much in summary – a defendant's rights come into play with the decision on legal aid, the various functions of the justices' clerk, the decision on venue, and the decisions of the court on disclosure, evidence, sentence and bail. The way in which the law is to be applied in these areas is set down in various acts, like the Magistrates Courts Act, the Bail Act, and the almost annual and increasingly draconian criminal justice provisions, as interpreted through case law. All of these decisions affect the fairness of the proceedings against the defendant and are therefore concerned with his rights – but almost none, apart from the Bail Act, adopt the language of rights.

The next section will look at the rights created (or expressed – depending on your point of view) by the HRA, whether the HRA has simply expressed the current position differently, and where new advances in individual's rights may most readily come.

SECTION 2
POSITION POST-HRA

Overview
The Convention rights and freedoms, as incorporated by the HRA, that are most directly relevant to the criminal process are: the prohibition on torture, including inhuman and degrading treatment; the right to liberty and security of the person; the right to a fair trial; the right to respect for private and family life; freedom of conscience and religion; freedom of expression; freedom of assembly and association. All the qualified rights are expressed in the same way: a broad statement of principle, which is then subject to various 'public interest' restrictions – to do with, for example, public health, morals or order.

All rights are to be secured without discrimination, and are also subject to Article 17 – the prohibition on the abuse of rights. This makes it clear that the Convention does not imply the right to engage in any activity aimed at the destruction or limitation of the rights and freedoms of others.

At first sight, then, the Convention is hardly revolutionary, as many of its rights are already established within the criminal law. As we have seen, the HRA has not altered the circumstances in which someone can be arrested under PACE or the common law – but the constitutional position is now expressed within Article 5 as a positive right to liberty and security, subject only to various qualifications, like lawful arrest.

Nevertheless, the HRA has started to have positive effects on 'making rights real'. In court and outside, it is assisting in developing a general political culture of rights – a belated shift from 'subject' to 'citizen'; in the courtroom, it is slowly leading to a new approach to the law; it has strengthened pro-defendant legal arguments that are commonly run, because European cases and opinions are now admissible; it is also starting to establish rights (particularly in relation to fair trial and privacy) that are under-developed.

Below, we look article by article at points which may well be successfully challenged under the HRA, and which may make a difference to the general rights of suspects, and the particular rights of suspects from minority communities.

In many ways, however, the strength of the HRA lies in its general approach – that, irrespective of precedent, the starting point of the criminal process is the range of rights within the Convention, which should be interpreted broadly, and are subject only to the exceptions laid down, which should be interpreted narrowly. It is the new approach to the construction of the law, of which proportionality is one principle, that will really make a difference – and this should be considered when thinking about the specific points dealt with below.

Most domestic law probably meets or exceeds the minimum standards of the Convention. Points are, however, likely to arise on the following issues, which may also crop up as topics for advice.

Article 3

Prohibition of Torture
This includes the right not to be subjected to inhuman or degrading treatment or punishment.

In this context, consider:

- Unnecessary use of handcuffs or intimate searches;
- Other allegations of serious police misconduct, to augment an application to exclude evidence, or as evidence that the police were not acting in the execution of their duty, or in a civil action against the police.

Article 5

The Right to Liberty and Security of the Person
This includes the right not to be deprived of liberty, except on lawful authority, properly exercised.

The Article also lays down requirements to inform a suspect promptly, in language he understands, of the reasons for his arrest and charge, and for his 'prompt' appearance before the court. It also deals with bail, and compensation for those arrested or detained in contravention of the provisions of the article.

In this context, consider:

- Whether the 'reasonable suspicion' test in PACE for search and arrest is too vague, ruling out the possibility of strict adherence – and so permits unjustified invasions of personal liberty and privacy on the basis of little more than an officer's 'hunch';
- Augmenting arguments on breach of PACE using the Convention – in s.78 applications, Police Act prosecutions and civil actions;
- Refusal of bail. Under Convention principles, a defendant must be released pending trial unless the state can show 'relevant and sufficient' reasons to justify his continued detention – and the case law is not quite identical with (and is more liberal than) the Bail Act provisions and approach. For example, it is debatable whether the power to remand in custody for a defendant's own welfare is compatible with the Convention. (The common magistrates' court practice of not giving a reasoned judgment, particularly in the grant of bail, and the Crown Court practice of hearing bail applications in the defendant's absence, may also be susceptible to challenge under Article 6 – see below).

Article 6

Right to a Fair Trial

This includes an entitlement to a fair and public hearing within a reasonable time by an independent and impartial tribunal established by law. It also lays down requirements for open justice; for the presumption of innocence; and for certain minimum rights for the defendant.

The defendant's minimum rights are: to be meaningfully informed in detail of the case against him; adequate time and facility for the preparation of his defence; to defend himself in person, through legal assistance of his own choosing, and to be given it free when the interest of justice so require; to examine or have examined witnesses against him and to obtain the attendance and the examination of witnesses on his behalf, under the same conditions as witnesses against him; to have the free assistance of an interpreter if he cannot understand or speak the language used in court.

In this context, consider:

- In the case of juveniles, whether youth court provisions afford them a fair trial;
- Whether the presumption of innocence is undermined by pre-trial publicity, or by charges that reverse the burden of proof, or that, implicitly, shift the burden of proof by requiring the defendant to answer questions. The CJPOA 'adverse inferences' from failure to answer questions, and the disclosure provisions which depend on the service of a defence statement, are also bound to be further challenged;

- In relation to the minimum rights, whether the defendant has had proper disclosure of the case against him, and of unused material that may assist his defence; whether he has had access to a solicitor, and has been granted or refused legal aid; whether evidence in suspect categories – for example, from accomplices, obtained by entrapment, or hearsay – has been admitted against him;
- Whether the court has acted impartially, particularly in the magistrates' court where, in certain default and enforcement proceedings, the clerk issues the summons and presents the case against the defendant – as well as advising the justices how to deal with an application.

Article 8

The Right to Respect for Private and Family Life

This includes the right to respect for private and family life, home and correspondence – qualified only by interference from a public authority in accordance with the law, and when necessary in a democratic society on various public interest grounds set out in Article 8(2).

In this context, consider:

- Whether intrusive surveillance will be a violation of Article 8 – and, if it is, whether the requirement of the fair trial under Article 6 requires that evidence obtained by unlawful telephone interception should be excluded.
- Whether the RIPA regime is compatible with Article 8 – especially in relation to the lack of judicial scrutiny of the decisions of the Secretary of State, or his various delegates – in the authorisation of intercept warrants.

Article 9

Freedom of Thought, Conscience and Religion

This Article includes the right to freedom of thought, conscience and religion – qualified only by limitations prescribed by law, and which are necessary in a democratic society in the interest of public safety, of the protection of public order, health or morals, or for the protection of the rights and freedoms of others. The ECtHR has held that Article 9 applies not only to religious beliefs but also to 'the conscientious beliefs of atheists, agnostics, sceptics, and the unconcerned' – and that pacifism is a belief within this section.

In this context, consider:

- Defences to offences arising from demonstrations.
- Defences of possession of cannabis by Rastafarians.

Article 10

Freedom of Expression

This includes the freedom to hold opinions and to receive and impart information and ideas without interference by public authority. It can be lawfully restricted, if necessary in a democratic society for various public interest reasons (like national security, prevention of crime, protection for the reputation or rights of others) which are specified, but widely drawn.

Importantly, it applies not only to information or ideas that are favourably received, or are regarded as inoffensive, but also to those that offend, shock or disturb the state or any sector of the population.

In this context, consider:

- The effect of proportionality in an Obscene Publications Act (or similar) prosecution; that is, where Article 10 rights are engaged, the justification for any criminal sanction must be convincingly established, and the question of proportionality is likely to be determined by the likely audience. (So that, for example, it probably is a breach of Article 10 to prosecute for showing an obscene film in a small projection room at the back of a sex shop – because it is unlikely that anyone would be confronted by the material by accident or against his will – but it might not be a breach to prosecute if the same material was on sale in a local video rental shop;
- The effect on prosecutions for inciting racial hatred, and whether the defendant's race would make a difference.

Article 11

Freedom of Assembly and Association

This includes the right to associate with others, including the right to form and join trade unions, again subject to restrictions prescribed by law and necessary in a democratic society in the interests of national security or public safety, for the prevention of crime or disorder, for the protection of health or morals, or the protection of the rights and freedoms of others.

In this context, consider:

- Whether a ban or the imposition of enforceable conditions on a *peaceful* demonstration, or a prosecution for a breach of that ban or conditions, will amount to a restriction – meaning it will have to be proportionate to be lawful.

Article 14

Prohibition of Discrimination
This is the right to enjoy all other Convention rights without discrimination on grounds such as sex, race, colour, language, religion, political or other opinion, national or social origin, association with the national minority, property, birth or other status. As explained in the Introduction, Article 14 has no independent existence. It does not establish a freestanding right to be free of discrimination, and relates only to the enjoyment of other Convention rights.

In this context, consider:

• Whether a breach of Article 5 on an improper 'stop and search' would also be a breach of Article 14 if the 'suspect' were black; in which case, studies showing that black people are stopped and searched without result far more than white people might be admissible.

SECTION 3

WHO CAN CLAIM?

A person who claims that a public authority has acted, or proposes to act, contrary to s.6(1) may bring proceedings against that public authority in the appropriate court or tribunal, or rely on the convention of right or rights in any legal proceedings – if they are (or would be) a 'victim' of an unlawful act.

In the criminal context, this clearly covers a suspect or defendant – but excludes applications from individuals not claiming to be affected themselves to stop interest groups bringing proceedings.

SECTION 4

WHO IS LIABLE?

Under the HRA, it is unlawful for a public authority to act in a manner incompatible with a Convention right. In this context, public authority includes the courts, the police, the CPS and Customs, and other public prosecuting authorities.

In crime, Convention rights will arise in the daily business before the criminal and divisional courts, which will be able to grant such relief as is 'just and appropriate' within their existing powers.

Challenges are likely to be mounted as a collateral challenge to a decision to prosecute; as a substantive defence to a common law charge; as an aid to construction of statutory offences; as an application for a declaration of incompatibility – as well as in the daily arguments about legal aid, bail and evidence.

SECTION 5

Case Study

Anna contacts you. She says that Billy, her son, was picked on, and beaten up by the police, who have charged him with assaulting a police constable in the execution of his duty. He has already been to the local Magistrates' Court, where the duty solicitor represented him. He has been refused bail – no reason was given. Anna doesn't feel comfortable with Billy's solicitor, who won't discuss the case with her.

Cliff, a friend who was with him, says that the police stopped him and wanted to search him because 'all you Rastafarians smoke drugs.' Cliff says another man, a passer by, saw it all, complained about police conduct, and insisted on giving his details to the police.

A trial date has been set for a couple of weeks' time. She doesn't know who will be called as witnesses.

She doesn't know what to do next. She feels that his human rights have been violated, and wonders if the HRA can help. She wants 'to do something.'

What do you do?

Questions for consideration

1. What does Anna actually want? (Information on whether she can do anything about Billy's charge before trial; the scope of Billy's entitlement to legal aid; what she can do about bail; general advice on the case, disclosure and procedure.)
2. What were the remedies on these particular issues prior to the HRA coming into force? Representations to the CPS on discontinuance: the Code for Crown Prosecutors; an application to the court to transfer legal aid to another firm: the Legal Aid Act 1988 and regulations; another bail application: the Bail Act; access to unused material.
3. Consider the application of the HRA. Are the police, CPS and court 'public authorities?' Yes – see above. Can Anna bring a claim? No – but Billy can, if he can show that the police, CPS or courts have acted incompatibly with his Convention rights.
4. What Convention rights are in issue? Potentially, Article 3 (inhuman

and degrading treatment); Article 5 (liberty and security); Article 6 (fair trial); Article 14 (prohibition on discrimination).

5. How can these rights be 'enforced' in this case? By augmenting existing applications or submissions – to, for example, the CPS to discontinue or for disclosure, or to the court to transfer legal aid, to grant bail, or find no case to answer because the officers were not acting in the execution of their duty – by reference to the approach laid down in the Convention, and European case law.

6. Would the HRA make a real difference on any of these points? As things stand, the CPIA (which regulates the disclosure of unused material) and the approach to bail commonly adopted in the Magistrates' Court are likely candidates for declarations of incompatibility. (The officer's remark about Rastafarians would be in breach of the Codes in any case, and could not possibly evidence a 'reasonable suspicion', even without Article 14.) . From the point of view of campaigning/publicity, mentioning 'human rights' might be a good way of mobilising support.

7. What practical steps should be taken? Check that Billy's wishes accord with those of his mother and that he wants her to be involved; pass on information/secure evidence that will assist him – like advising him to see a doctor to get his injuries documented, passing on Cliff's details to the solicitor, making sure the solicitor knows about the other potential witness so disclosure can be chased.

Education

Philip Engelman

The principal Article of the Convention concerning education is Article 2 of Protocol 1. This provides that 'No person shall be denied the right to education. In the exercise of any functions which it assumes in relation to education and teaching, the State shall respect the right of parents to ensure such education and teaching in conformity with their own religious and philosophical convictions'.

The UK was a signatory to the Treaty under which the Convention was made. However, it maintained a reservation, which is set out in the HRA as follows: '... In view of certain provisions of the Education Acts in the UK, the principle affirmed in the second sentence of Article 2 is accepted by the UK only so far as it is compatible with the provision of efficient instruction and training, and the avoidance of unreasonable public expenditure'.

Article 14 provides that 'The enjoyment of the rights and freedoms set forth in this Convention shall be secured without discrimination on any ground such as sex, race, colour, language, religion, political or other opinion, national or social origin, association with a national minority, property, birth or other status'.

In addition, Articles 6, 8 and 9 of the Convention may be of relevance.

SECTION 1
POSITION PRE-HRA

Before incorporation of the Convention, the central education-related rights were conferred by the Education Acts and, in addition, the SSFA. The Education Acts relate to admissions to schools, exclusions from schools and schools reorganisations. There are also parental rights relating to school transport and special educational needs.

This chapter does not deal with parental rights in relation to the acquisition of foundation (previously grant-maintained) status, nor with the rights of petitioning for a ballot and voting in that ballot in relation to grammar schools, the latter conferred by the SSFA.

Non-Discrimination

There is a general duty on the part of Local Education Authorities (or LEAs, which largely administer state education), the governing bodies of all state schools, the proprietors of independent schools, and the governing bodies of all colleges and universities, not to discriminate against any person in relation to admissions, access to any benefits, exclusion or subjection to any detriment. This duty arises out of s.17 RRA. In addition, LEAs must not discriminate on racial grounds in any of their other functions (for example, general admissions policies or prosecuting parents whose children truant from school): s.18 RRA.

Other institutions and organisations in the public and private sectors that provide vocational training are prohibited from discriminating under s.13 RRA.

In addition, discrimination by the Further and Higher Education Funding Council is outlawed by the RRA (by way of amendment inserted by the FHEA). Also outlawed is any discrimination by the Teacher Training Agency and the Learning and Skills Council.

Section 19B RRA, inserted by the RR(A)A, prohibits public authorities from doing any act which constitutes discrimination in the carrying out of their functions. The concept of a 'public authority' is defined as including 'any person certain of whose functions are of a public nature'. Private acts performed by public authorities are excluded. Public authorities will undoubtedly include all the bodies referred to above, save that the proprietors of independent schools are not, in the writer's view, a public authority.

The sanction for a breach of the duties set out in ss.17 and 19B is an entitlement to bring civil proceedings in the County Court. All the usual remedies that are obtainable in the High Court are available. These include damages, declaratory and injunctive relief. Notice must be given of such a claim to the Secretary of State.

Under the new s.71 RRA, inserted by the RR(A)A, there is a duty, not only upon local authorities and LEAs, but also upon the governing bodies of all maintained schools and of all publicly funded colleges and universities, to carry out their function with due regard to the need (a) to eliminate unlawful racial discrimination; and (b) to promote equality of opportunity and good relations between persons of different racial groups. This is a harder-edged provision than the earlier version of s.71, which related only to local authorities. It is of wider ambit.

Educational bodies are also required to prepare a race equality policy and to assess the impact of its policies (and also monitor them) on pupils, staff and parents of different racial groups, including, in particular, the impact on attainment levels of pupils. This duty is imposed on the governing bodies of educational establishments maintained by LEAs and the governing bodies of various colleges. The governing institutions of those in the further and higher education sector also have a duty to monitor the admission and progress of students and the recruitment and career progress of staff.

The Home Secretary's order (as discussed in Chapter 2, above) requires governing bodies of LEA maintained educational establishments to prepare a race equality policy and to assess the impact of its policies (and also monitor them) on pupils, staff and parents of different racial groups, particularly in connection with pupils' attainment levels. The governing bodies of publicly funded colleges and universities are required to prepare a race equality policy and to monitor the admission and progress of students and the recruitment and career progress of staff. The code of practice which the CRE has issued applies to LEAs and to the governing bodies of schools, colleges and universities.

Where the CRE is of the view that a public authority is failing to comply with the Home Secretary's order, it can serve a Compliance Notice. That Notice can be enforced in the County Court. The only form of enforcement of breach of duty imposed specifically on a public authority is by way of enforcement proceedings by the CRE.

Breach of the Section 71 general duty may also attract judicial review remedies. For example, if an LEA decides to close a school, or a college decides to reorganise its curriculum, and in doing they fail to take account of the impact of that decision on different racial groups, any person or group likely to be affected could challenge the decision in a claim for judicial review.

Application of the domestic principle of non-discrimination

An important leading case is *Mandla v Dowell Lee* [1983] 2 AC 548. There, when examining the duty under s.17 RRA, the House of Lords held that it was unlawful indirect discrimination for a school to refuse admission to a pupil on the grounds that he was wearing a turban.

The various cases on school re-organisation, which substantially relate to differential treatment on the grounds of sex, have also demonstrated that the principles of racial equality will be applicable to such re-organisation.

The courts have also considered the application of s.18 RRA to the duty to have regard to parental preference in relation to admissions to schools.

The Court of Appeal has held that the parental preference under the EA is not qualified or overridden by the s.18 duty; see *R v Cleveland County Council ex parte Commission for Racial Equality* (1992) Times 25 August.

One should also note that there is no absolute duty to educate children in accordance with their parents' wishes.

School admissions

The SSFA, which governs the right of parents to state a preference for the school at which they wish their child to be educated, is not absolute. It is subject to the following exceptions:

- Where compliance with a preference would prejudice the provision of efficient education or the efficient use of resources;
- Where compliance for a preference with a foundation or voluntary aided school would be incompatible with any special arrangements made for admission to that school;
- Where the schools admission arrangements are based on ability or aptitude and compliance with a preference would be incompatible with selection under these arrangements;
- Where compliance with the preference would jeopardise the duty of the LEA and the Governing Body to comply with limits on infant class sizes;
- Where the admission arrangements for two or more maintained schools provided for co-ordinated admissions; and
- Where the child has been permanently excluded from two or more schools.

The essence of this right confers upon the parents of children the right to express a preference as to the school at which their child should be educated, and the duty upon the LEA to comply with that preference unless one of the circumstances in which the preference can be disapplied exists. The most important aspect of this right is that it applies whether or not the parent resides within the LEA Area.

In one case on the admissions policy of local authorities, it was held that a catchment area did not discriminate against the Asian minority, because it was the area and not the ethnic background of the parent that was relevant. One wonders whether the same decision would be reached where stronger evidence was available as to the 'pool' in the relevant catchment area.

It is also significant to note that it is lawful for a state aided school to have admissions criteria which are intended to preserve the character of the school. This allows religion to play a part in the selection policy for such a school.

There is a right of appeal in relation to state schools to the Education Appeal Committee. That Appeal Committee is bound to give reasons for its decision. There is, however, a restriction on the right of appeal in relation to admissions to infant classes.

Different rules apply to children with statements of special educational needs and those in respect of whom a School Attendance Order has been made.

School expulsions

The statutory framework contemplates that any decision taken in respect of expulsion by the Head Teacher of a state school is subject to a right of appeal. The rules of natural justice apply to the hearing of such an appeal. The principles of non-discrimination also apply. In relation to private schools, there can be no judicial review of such a decision because the statutory framework does not apply to such a school. There will be remedies in the private law of contract and it is likely that the same rules of natural justice will apply. Further, the duty not to discriminate unlawfully imposed by the RRA will apply to the proprietors of such a school.

School reorganisation

The golden thread running through reorganisations of state schools (i.e. the closure, opening or amalgamation of schools) is the right on the part of the parents to be consulted by the LEA. Case law has established that the only legal obligation upon an LEA in relation to consultation is to consult in English: *R v Birmingham City Council ex p Kaur* (1991) 155 L.G.Rev 587. The non- discrimination duty under the RRA also undoubtedly applies.

School transport

The basic rule in relation to school transport is that, if a pupil's parents live more than 3 miles from the school (or 2 miles if the child is under 6), then free school transport is available. There are a number of cases on the meaning of '3 miles': in general, it means not as the 'crow flies', but the safest walking route. The provisions of s.17 RRA will apply to the provision of free school transport.

Special educational needs

A child has a 'special educational need' if he or she has a learning difficulty, meaning a significantly greater difficulty in learning than the majority of children of his or her age (see s.312 EA). A child whose special educational needs are such that he or she requires 'special educational provision' beyond that generally provided in schools in his or her area is entitled to a 'Statement of Special Educational Needs'. There are procedures for assessment and the making of a statement. An appeal against the making or non-making of a statement lies to the Special Educational Needs Tribunal.

As the making or the non-making of a statement is a function of the LEA, the non-discrimination provisions of the RRA will apply.

SECTION 2
POSITION POST-HRA

Overview
The most obvious manner in which the Convention affects education involves the inter-relationship between the Article 2 of Protocol 1 (the right to education referred to above) and Article 14, the non-discrimination provision. Articles 6, 8 and 9 may also be of relevance.

Principal cases
The principal ECtHR cases relating to the right to education are:

* The *Belgian Linguistic* case, which establishes that parents have no right to their child to be educated in the family's language, only a right of access to the school providing education in one of the national languages;
* The *Kjeldsen v Denmark* case, which establishes that parents of children are not entitled to withdraw them from lessons concerning sex education;
* The *Campbell and another v UK* case, which establishes that objections can be made to corporal punishment at UK state schools that is contrary to parents' philosophical convictions; and
* The *Valsamis v Greece* case, which establishes that, although parents are entitled to respect for their religious convictions, they are not entitled to refuse to permit their child to take part in a school parade on a national holiday, which parade was attended by the military.

Article 3

Prohibition of torture
It has been held that the threat of corporal punishment does *not* constitute inhuman or degrading treatment contrary to Article 3: *Campbell etc v UK*.

Article 6

Right to a Fair Trial
The Article 6 right to a fair hearing has been successfully invoked in a case

where English teachers wished to open a language school in Greece, but were delayed by the Greek authorities. However, an LEA's decision on choice of a school for a dyslexic child did not take place in circumstances affecting the parents' rights under Article 6. In any event, such a decision would be subject to review by the Special Educational Needs Tribunal.

The courts have recently considered the question of whether Article 6 applies to cases of exclusion for misconduct (*R v Head Teacher of Alperton Community School*). It was held that Article 6 did not apply.

Article 8

The Right to Respect for Private and Family Life

It is possible that this Article could be invoked in relation to religious beliefs. However, in the case of *Angelini v Sweden*, the ECtHR held that it is not a breach of the Convention to require the child of an atheist to attend a course of religious knowledge. In fact, s.13 HRA specifically preserves the exercise by a religious organisation (whether by itself or its members) of the Convention's right to freedom of thought, conscience and religion.

This provision was considered in relation to school admissions and the 'sibling' rule in two recent cases. In one (*R v St James' RC School Appeal Panel*), the Court held that Article 8 conferred no absolute right to have a child admitted to a school already attended by a sibling. However, in another (*R v South Gloucestershire Appeal Panel*), the Court reserved the question of whether an admission criterion giving preference to some siblings (on proximity grounds), but denied to others, was in breach of Article 8.

Article 14

Prohibition of Discrimination

The general prohibition of discrimination has been explored in the *Belgian Linguistic* case (see above), where it was held that it was a breach of Article 14 to permit Dutch-speaking families to have access to schools that were barred to French-speaking families.

Possibly the most useful area of interaction between Article 14 and existing law on racial discrimination is in relation to actual or potentially discriminatory admissions policies. The central question is the applicability of s.18 RRA, requiring that an LEA does not do any racially discriminatory act in carrying out its Education Act duties. As noted above, this was held in the *Cleveland County Council* case not to override the concept of 'parental preference', now set out in the SSFA.

It is difficult to see how the *Cleveland County Council* decision can be right, and its lack of logic is reinforced further under the HRA, when a combination of the non-denial of the right to education and the prohibition on discrimination will be effective. It is likely that, in any future challenge based on the collision between the principles of non-discrimination and 'parental preference', a different result would now be reached.

The 1994 case of *R v Lancashire County Council ex parte F* upholds a decision whereby preference is given to non-Catholics above Catholics when considering selection into state schools. If one were to translate that decision from Catholicism into Sikhism, one wonders whether it would still be good law under the provisions of the HRA.

One wonders whether the decisions of the ECtHR on non-subsidisation of private schools (see above) might be reconsidered, for example in relation to the subsidisation of a Muslim School. Perhaps not, but the possibility remains.

One also wonders whether the distinction between fees paid by home students and overseas students – see *Orphanos v Queen Mary College* (1985) – would withstand the Article 2 and Article 14 duties.

Article 2 of Protocol 1

The Right to Education

The central question raised by Article 2 of Protocol 1 is this: what does the phrase 'no person shall be denied the right to education' actually mean?

In the *Belgian Linguistic* case, the ECtHR held that it contained a positive obligation on the State to the extent that regulation 'must never injure the substance of the right to education nor conflict with other Convention rights'. However, it was also established in that case that there is no obligation on the part of the State to subsidise private schools. This view has been echoed in domestic law and the UK courts have refused to find any potential conflict between the right set out in Article 2 of Protocol 1 and the abolition of the Assisted Places scheme and, most recently, the differential drawn between those entitled to vote in grammar school ballots.

The right set out in Article 2 of Protocol 1 does not permit parents in this country to insist on single-sex grammar schools. Nor does it permit overseas students' immigration into the UK for the purposes of receiving UK education. However, it has been held, again in the *Belgian Linguistic* case, that privately educated children are entitled to have the results of their education recognised by the State.

In respect of children who have special educational needs, it has been held that Article 2 of Protocol 1 does not entitle the parents of a disabled child to a insist upon a place in a mainstream school, because of their philosophical convictions, where there has been an offer of a special school. It has also been held that an LEA is not bound to pay for the cost of transport of a statemented child to a school of the parents' choice.

It has recently been held (in *R v London Borough of Newham*) that the provisions of Article 2 Protocol 1 could assist a Muslim parent seeking the admission of his daughter to a school on the grounds of religious beliefs by requiring the LEA to give due weight to his religious convictions.

SECTION 3
WHO CAN CLAIM?

The parents of a child, where that child is under 18, usually have the right under the above legislation; thus, any breach of those rights entitles the parents of the child to bring proceedings under the HRA. However, I take the view that a child is also able to bring proceedings as a 'victim' under the provisions of the HRA. This issue is of particular importance given a recent decision of the Court of Appeal that generally Legal Aid should be refused to a child where a parent was able to bring proceedings.

SECTION 4
WHO IS LIABLE?

Central government, the relevant Secretary of State, LEAs and the governing bodies of state schools, colleges and universities are all 'public authorities' within the meaning of the HRA and are thus bound not to act in a way incompatible with Convention rights. This probably extends to the Governors of a Private School when they discharge functions under the Education Acts, possibly save in respect of expulsion (see *R v Fernhill Manor Place School ex parte A* (1993) 1 FLR 620).

It is very unlikely that an individual teacher in a state school constitutes a 'public authority' within the meaning of the HRA. However, this issue poses no problem, because the LEA or the governing body will be vicariously liable for the teachers as employees of the school in question.

SECTION 5

Case Study
Mrs A has written to the LEA asking her son to be transferred from the Council's School at X Road, which has a large number of black pupils, to

Y School, which is predominantly white. The LEA agreed to the mother's request. The Commission for Racial Equality applied for a declaration that the LEA committed an act of discrimination, contrary to s.18 RRA, by transferring the child between X and Y Schools.

1. Was the LEA obliged under the pre-HRA law to comply with the mother's request under the doctrine of 'parental preference'?
2. Do the provisions of the Convention affect your answer?

Immigration law

Ramby De Mello and Judith Farbey

This chapter looks at how the HRA has had an impact in terms of racial discrimination issues affecting immigration control.

SECTION 1

POSITION PRE-HRA

First, it is helpful to have an understanding of the general framework governing immigration control.

How does the UK control immigration?

Immigration control lies in the discretion of the Secretary of State for the Home Department.

The Secretary of State's discretion is subject to:

- Statutes: The main statutes are currently the IA and the IAA.
- Secondary legislation: Statutory instruments are used to deal with an increasingly wide range of issues. The IAA is notable for its dependency on statutory instruments that are not subject to the same Parliamentary scrutiny as primary legislation.

  There are regulations setting down the circumstances in which a person who is subject to a negative Home Office decision must be given notice to that effect in writing. Regulations also set out who may appeal to the Immigration Appellate Authority if refused a visa to visit family members in the UK.
- Immigration Rules: The Rules are a basic tool for making immigration decisions. They are set down in House of Commons Papers that must be laid before Parliament. The current rules are contained in HC 395.

  In essence, the Rules set out the criteria that different categories of person must meet in order to enter or remain in the UK. The categories include visitors, students, workers, family members, asylum seekers and certain others. The Rules also set down general grounds on which a person may be refused a visa, or leave to enter or remain in the UK. They deal with criteria and procedures for deportation and removal from the UK.

- Policy statements: The Home Office will sometimes issue a policy statement that it will treat certain kinds of cases outside the Immigration Rules. For example, the Home Office may decide that it is too dangerous to remove anyone from the UK to a particular country at war and so announce in a policy statement that it will allow all nationals of that country to remain in the UK for a limited period, on an exceptional basis.
- Immigration Directorate Instructions: These are detailed instructions to Home Office caseworkers about how to apply the Immigration Rules and how to exercise discretion outside the Rules. They are available on the Home Office's website.
- Exercise of discretion in individual cases: The Home Office has a duty to look at each case on its facts. Subject to statutory restraints, the Home Office can exercise discretion, in favour of an individual, outside rules, policies and instructions. Discretion can be exercised at any stage and irrespective of a previous adverse immigration decision.

In addition, the UK is a signatory to various international treaties and conventions, such as the 1951 Convention Relating to the Status of Refugees. The UK is also a signatory to European Union agreements that govern freedom of movement for citizens of EU nations.

Who is subject to immigration control?
Only those who have a 'right of abode' in the UK can enter and remain in the UK at will. The main group of people with a right of abode are British citizens, who are not subject to immigration control.

Those who do not have a right of abode in the UK:

- have to obtain permission to enter and remain in the UK; and
- may be removed from the UK if they fall into a particular category.

There are three main categories of people who may be removed from the UK:

- Overstayers who have remained in the UK beyond the period of their leave to stay;

- Illegal entrants; and
- Those whose presence in the UK is not conducive to the public good, such as convicted criminals.

Immigration officers have power to admit persons into the UK temporarily while their cases are being decided. Temporary admission is not a form of immigration status – it is simply admission onto the territory for the purpose of dealing with an application to enter or stay in the UK or to stop removal.

European Union citizens may come and work and even reside in the UK providing they are self-sufficient. They remain, ultimately, subject to immigration control.

Who carries out immigration control?
Immigration control is exercised at three different points:

- Entry clearance: Many people who wish to enter the UK require a visa, known in legal language as an entry clearance. Entry Clearance Officers are posted abroad in British High Commissions and Embassies and deal with all applications for entry clearance to enter the UK.
- Leave to enter: An entry clearance does not guarantee entry to the UK. Immigration Officers are situated in the various ports and airports in the UK and are responsible for granting permission to enter the UK. An Immigration Officer may refuse someone leave to enter even if that person has an entry clearance, for example if the Immigration Officer takes the view that the person's circumstances have changed since the entry clearance was issued.
- Leave to remain: The Home Office's Immigration and Nationality Directorate is responsible for deciding who can extend their stay after the initial leave to enter has expired. The Immigration and Nationality Department staff will carry out their duties without regard to the race, colour or religion of persons seeking to enter or remain in the UK. This duty is set out in the Immigration Rules.

Refugees
Many people are forced to flee on an involuntary basis because it is no longer safe for them to remain in their own country. They seek protection in the UK. The UK is a signatory to the 1951 Convention Relating to the Status of Refugees (as amended by the 1967 Protocol Relating to the Status of Refugees). Those who satisfy the refugee definition under the Convention are recognised as refugees and granted refugee status.

The refugee definition is set out in Article 1(A)(2) of the Convention. In brief, a refugee is a person who has 'a well-founded fear of being perse-cuted for reasons of race, religion, nationality, membership of a particular social group or political opinion'.

A person who is recognised as a refugee in the UK is currently granted indefinite leave to remain, also known as settlement.

Taking the main elements of the definition:

- Fear: A person must demonstrate a genuine fear of return to his or her own country. This does not mean that an asylum applicant must demon-strate any particular psychological state or reaction. Rather, it means that the applicant must demonstrate genuine alienation from country of origin and that continued stay in that country has become intolerable. The fear element is subjective: it is assessed by reference to an appli-cant's own statements about his or her reasons for fleeing to the UK.
- Well-founded: The applicant's fear must be well-founded in the sense that it must be supported by the objective situation in the country of origin. The Home Office gathers country information from a variety of governmental and non-governmental sources, which its case workers can utilise when making decisions.
- Persecution: An asylum applicant must have a well-founded fear of persecution. The concept of persecution is key to the Refugee Convention. The English courts have kept its meaning flexible, so that it can cover numerous kinds of ill treatment, reflecting the multiple ways in which human beings can harm each other. It can be broadly defined as 'persistent and serious ill treatment'. Loss of liberty or serious physi-cal ill treatment will usually be regarded as persecution.

  Persecution does not usually include the generalised effects of civil war. Nor does it cover those who are simply fleeing from criminal pros-ecution. Discrimination may not amount to persecution. However, where the discrimination is serious and substantially prejudicial to the victim, it may amount to persecution. In this way, those who are victims of seri-ous racial or religious discrimination may qualify for refugee status.

  A person may be persecuted by the State or by non-State actors, such as sections of the populace or powerful terrorist groups. Where the persecutor is a non-State actor, the asylum applicant must demonstrate that the State is unwilling or unable to provide adequate protection from persecution.

  Application of the Refugee Convention involves a prospective analy-sis of risk: the question is whether someone will be at risk of persecution in the future. A person who has never suffered persecution may be recognised as a refugee because he or she can demonstrate a risk of suffering persecution in future. Conversely, if a person has suffered persecution in the past, but cannot demonstrate a risk of suffering persecution in future, the fear of persecution will not be well-founded and refugee status will be denied. Nevertheless, the courts have held that past persecution is a good indicator of future risk.

The risk of persecution need not extend to the whole country, but a person may be denied refugee status if it is reasonable for him or her to relocate within the country. The current test in English law is whether it would be 'unduly harsh' for a person to utilise an internal flight alternative.

Under the Convention definition, persecution must be related to one of five grounds:

- Race
- Religion
- Nationality
- Membership of a particular social group
- Political opinion

Even if someone is at risk of serious ill treatment such as torture, he or she is not a refugee if the ill treatment will be inflicted for a reason other than those set down in the Refugee Convention. Such persons would probably qualify for exceptional leave to remain in the UK, on a compassionate basis. Exceptional leave to remain is leave to remain granted outside the Immigration Rules and at the discretion of the Home Office.

The Refugee Convention imposes a fundamental duty to avoid 'refoulement'. Refoulement means the expulsion of a refugee to the frontiers of territories where his or her life or freedom would be threatened for one of the reasons set down in the Refugee Convention.

The Refugee Convention treats some people as undeserving of protection. These people are excluded from the protection of the Refugee Convention: even if they are refugees, they need not be granted refugee status. Exclusion clauses apply to those who have:

- committed a crime against peace, a war crime, or a crime against humanity, as defined in the international instruments drawn up to make provision for such crimes;
- committed a serious non-political crime outside the country of refuge;
- been guilty of acts contrary to the purposes and principles of the United Nations.

These exclusion categories reflect the historical background of the Refugee Convention, which was drawn up in the aftermath of the Second World War when the international community was arguably trying to promote a certain moral view around such institutions as the United Nations. Those who were regarded as outside the pale, in moral terms, were to be excluded from protection.

The Home Office has no duty to consider an asylum claim on its merits if there is a safe third country to which the asylum claimant can be sent. Under the IAA, all EU member States are deemed to be safe third countries. The Dublin Convention sets out criteria for determining which EU member State has responsibility for dealing with an asylum claim. When the Home Office considers that one of the Dublin Convention criteria apply, it will request the relevant EU State to accept responsibility for dealing with the asylum claim. Once the EU member State has agreed to deal with the asylum claim, it is very difficult to challenge a decision to remove the asylum seeker to that member State.

Challenging adverse immigration decisions

In many instances, adverse decisions from the Home Office or from Entry Clearance Officers abroad can be challenged before the Immigration Appellate Authority. The appeal rights are set down in statute. There are three tiers set down in the IAA:

- Adjudicator
- Immigration Appeal Tribunal (IAT)
- Court of Appeal.

The IAA does not deal with appeal to the House of Lords, but this lies in the normal way.

In certain circumstances, appeal lies only to an adjudicator and the case cannot progress to the IAT. In all cases, appeal to the IAT lies only with leave to appeal from the Tribunal. Appeal to the Court of Appeal lies with leave to appeal from the IAT or the Court of Appeal. The IAA sets down that appeal to the Court of Appeal is limited to questions of law.

Where there is no statutory right of appeal, resort may be had to judicial review proceedings. However, judicial review proceedings are limited to questions of law, whereas appeals to adjudicators and to the IAT can cover factual as well as legal questions.

Dealing with racial discrimination in an immigration context

Under RR(A)A, it is unlawful for immigration officials to discriminate against a person on grounds of race or colour. However, it is not unlawful for officials taking immigration decisions to discriminate on grounds of nationality or ethnic or national origin where this is authorised by a government minister or required by immigration legislation or rules.

There is ministerial authorisation to treat people differently by reason of their nationality if there is statistical or intelligence information showing that persons of that nationality breach the immigration laws. The different treatment that is permitted includes the power to subject persons to a more rigorous examination than other persons in the same circumstances.

Complaints of racial discrimination against immigration officials attract a right of appeal to an adjudicator, and then to the IAT. The complaint must relate to an immigration decision. Complaints relating solely to the general conduct of immigration officials are dealt with in a County Court under non-immigration legislation. If an adjudicator or the IAT finds that a person has suffered discrimination in relation to an immigration decision, their findings can be referred to a County Court which will determine what damages should be awarded to the applicant.

SECTION 2

POSITION POST-HRA

As with other chapters, the pre-HRA framework remains in place following the coming into force of the HRA. But what difference has the HRA made?

As mentioned above, not all those who fear ill treatment in their own country qualify as refugees. Prior to the HRA, the Immigration Appellate Authority had jurisdiction to consider refugee issues but had no jurisdiction to consider broader human rights issues. This was perceived to be a problematic lacuna in immigration legislation. Consequently, under s.65 HRA, the Immigration Appellate Authority was given jurisdiction to consider immigration decisions within the context of the HRA.

Taking the main elements of s.65:

- The section covers decisions taken by the Home Office, Immigration Officers and Entry Clearance Officers.
- The decision must relate to a person's 'entitlement to enter or remain in the United Kingdom'. Thus, section 65 does not cover decisions relating to detention under immigration powers.
- In order to trigger the appeal right, a person who is subject to an adverse immigration decision must 'allege' that his or her human rights have been breached. The allegation is best made in a letter to the relevant immigration official.
- Adjudicators and the IAT have jurisdiction to allow an appeal on the basis that the immigration official has breached a person's human rights by taking a decision that is made unlawful under the HRA.

In practice, there are two main ways in which adjudicators and the IAT consider human rights issues, and these relate to Articles 3 and 8.

Article 3

Prohibition of Torture

The UK will breach Article 3 if it expels a person to a place where he or she will suffer treatment prohibited by Article 3 (torture, inhuman or degrading treatment or punishment).

The Immigration Appellate Authority has jurisdiction to determine whether expulsion would give rise to a breach; it must decide whether there are substantial grounds for believing that a person faces a real risk of treatment prohibited by Article 3.

The Immigration Appellate Authority's jurisdiction to allow an appeal on Article 3 grounds gives benefits to:

- Those who will suffer ill treatment if expelled from the UK but who cannot demonstrate that the ill treatment will be inflicted for one of the reasons set down under the Refugee Convention.
- Those who are refugees but do not qualify for refugee status because the Refugee Convention regards them as undeserving of protection (as set out above). However, some of those deemed undeserving of refugee status will also be considered a threat to the UK on national security or political grounds. These people have no right of appeal to the Immigration Appellate Authority, but have appeal rights to the Special Immigration Appeals Commission whose workings are beyond the scope of this chapter.

Article 8

Right to Respect for Private and Family Life

The most frequent resort to Article 8 in the immigration context is where a person seeks to avoid expulsion from the UK on the basis of marriage to a British citizen or person settled in the UK. Even where a marriage is genuine, Article 8(2) allows decision-makers to balance respect for family life against the interests of the enforcement of immigration control.

In *R on the application of Mahmood v Secretary of State for the Home Department* [2001] INLR 1, the Court of Appeal set down some principles which in practice guide the Immigration Appellate Authority in carrying out this balancing exercise:

- The UK has a right under the Convention to control the entry of non-nationals into its territory.

- Article 8 does not impose a general obligation on the UK to respect the choice of country of residence of a married couple.
- Removal of one family member from the UK will not necessarily breach Article 8 provided that there are no insurmountable obstacles to other family members living together in the country of origin of the family member who is to be expelled, even where this involves a degree of hardship for the other family members.
- Article 8 is likely to be violated by the expulsion of person who has been long established in the UK if it is not reasonable to expect other members of the family to follow.
- Knowledge on the part of one spouse at the time of marriage that rights of residence of the other were precarious militates against a finding that expulsion violates Article 8.
- Whether interference with family rights is justified in the interests of controlling immigration will depend on (i) the facts of the particular case and (ii) the circumstances prevailing in the State whose action is impugned.

Against this background, an applicant may have to demonstrate why it is unreasonable for the Home Office to require him or her to return to the country of origin and obtain entry clearance as a spouse from there. The courts have accepted that the government can reasonably expect someone to return to the country of origin to obtain entry clearance, rather than 'jump the queue' by being granted spouse status here.

A person who is successful on a human rights appeal will be granted exceptional leave to remain in the UK, usually for four years.

In so far as it was possible to raise human rights in judicial review proceedings prior to the commencement of the HRA, the impact of the HRA in the immigration context may be less than in other areas of law. However, the human rights appeal is a welcome addition – it provides a factual forum for the adjudication of human rights issues that was not available before.

SECTION 3

WHO CAN CLAIM?

In principal, any individual wishing to challenge a public authority decision in the immigration context can bring a claim, including of course those applying for asylum in the UK.

SECTION 4

WHO IS LIABLE?

Central government, the relevant Secretary of State and the immigration authorities are all 'public authorities' within the meaning of the HRA and are thus bound not to act in a way incompatible with Convention rights.

SECTION 5

Case Study

Mahdi is an Iranian national who arrived in the UK in October 2000. He claims to fear persecution from the Iranian government because he has been active in the pro-democracy movement in Iran. He has been arrested and detained twice. Mahdi claims asylum.

Unfortunately, two years later, the Secretary of State for the Home Department rejects his asylum application on the basis that, although he may have been persecuted in the past, he does not face persecution in the future. In the meantime, Mahdi has married a British citizen who has three children by a previous marriage and sole care of her elderly mother. Mahdi's wife also works part time for a charity assisting blind people.

1. What appeal rights does Mahdi have to an adjudicator?
2. What kind of information should Mahdi obtain in order to satisfy the adjudicator that the Secretary of State was wrong to reject his asylum claim?
3. How might you go about persuading an adjudicator that his expulsion from the UK would breach Article 8 of the Convention? In particular, how might you persuade an adjudicator that Mahdi should not be expected to return to Iran simply to obtain entry clearance as a spouse?
4. If Mahdi loses his appeal to an adjudicator, what other steps could you take to assist him?
5. Would it make any difference if:

   (a) Mahdi, on his way from Iran to the UK, had spent three years in France where he had committed a serious drugs offence; or
   (b) Mahdi had, since his arrival in the UK, contracted a debilitating disease?

A final word of warning: at time of writing, immigration and asylum issues are a political hot potato and look as if they will remain so for some time. As a result, the pace of legal change is fast and the statutory framework for immigration control is increasingly complex. General principles are almost inevitably subject to exceptions. The above, broad framework can act only as a guide and, it is hoped, as a temptation to more specialist reading.

Racism and freedom of expression

Geoffrey Bindman

This chapter considers the impact of the HRA on issues of freedom of expression.

SECTION 1

POSITION PRE-HRA

As is the case with other rights protected by the HRA, the right to freedom of expression contained in Article 10 of the Convention previously had no clear cut existing protection in the domestic law of the UK. Although there was a long tradition of claiming a right to free speech, it existed – like so many other rights in our common law – only to the extent that there was no contrary restriction. In this sense, there was a right to do anything that the law did not prohibit. There were also a few statutory provisions protecting freedom of expression in specific situations; for example, s.10 CCA gives some protection to journalists from attempts to force them to reveal sources of information.

Law of defamation

Previously, the best-known restriction on freedom of expression was imposed by the law of defamation (for most purposes, the word 'libel' is interchangeable). This provides remedies both civil and criminal (though criminal libel is rarely prosecuted) where a statement published about someone is claimed to cause damage to reputation. The defendant – usually the publisher or author of the material complained of – can defend the claim by proving that the statement is true, or, if it is a comment honestly believed on a matter of public interest, can plead 'fair comment'. This has become increasingly relied on by the media and is accepted by the courts as a sufficient defence to a libel claim when the defendant has made reasonable efforts to check the facts, even though what is published is not in fact accurate.

Defamation and racism

Defamation (or libel) of course can occur in many cases that have nothing to do with race or discrimination but there have been cases in which racism has been the central issue. It is obviously defamatory to call someone a racist and some of those accused of racism have successfully sued for libel. Ray Honeyford, the former Bradford teacher, and Roger Scruton, the philosopher, are examples. In a more recent libel action in which racism has featured, the far right-wing historian, David Irving, notoriously sued the author and publishers of a book which accused him of being an anti-semite, a Hitler partisan, and a bogus historian. The defendants said the allegations were true and the court ruled in their favour.

Legal aid is not available for libel actions but lawyers are now allowed to take cases on a 'no win, no fee' basis (see the chapter below on Obtaining and Funding Legal Assistance). This means that accusations of racism against individuals or commercial organisations can be risky in the absence of clear proof that the accusation is justified. Remember that the maker of a defamatory statement has, if sued, the burden of justifying it.

Other restrictions on free expression

Public use of threatening, abusive and insulting language may amount to a criminal offence under legislation designed to protect the public from disorder and violence. This law, now contained in the POA, originated in the need to curb the violent activities of the fascist demagogue Sir Oswald Mosley and his supporters in the 1930s. More recently, it has been extended to create offences of inciting racial hatred, and the possession or distribution of racially inflammatory material. Prosecutions still require the consent of the Attorney General and some holders of that office have been very reluctant to use their powers, partly because of weaknesses in the drafting of the law that have made it difficult to secure convictions in some cases. Nevertheless there has been increasing willingness to prosecute very recently and the police should be pressed to investigate any such activity.

There are other laws which also, to some extent, bring the criminal law to bear on racist behaviour. Although not mentioning race explicitly they could be used to curb racist behaviour and there are indications that prosecuting authorities are prepared to use these laws to target racism. Among them are the ObPA, the TA, the MCA and the FOA. There are also offences of harassment under ss.4 and 5 of the POA.

The PHA, expanding on ss.4 and 5 of the POA, makes it an offence to pursue a course of conduct amounting to harassment – without defining harassment. However, it includes conduct that alarms or causes distress, and it may be committed by speech and causing fear of violence, and this adds to the possible penalties. When sentencing a person convicted of an offence under the PHA, the court may also issue a restraining order to protect the victim from further harassment or fear of violence. Breach of a restraining order is of course also an offence and a serious one punishable by imprisonment up to five years.

The CDA strengthens the impact of these and other provisions of the criminal law on racist activity by introducing enhanced penalties where a crime is racially aggravated. Where an offender demonstrates racial hostility towards the victim of the offence or the offence is motivated by racial hostility, higher penalties than those otherwise prescribed may be imposed. This applies to offences of violence and also harassment under the PHA or the POA.

The offences created by all this complicated legislation cover much activity beyond speech and expression but they provide opportunities for the prosecution of those who spread racial hatred through speech and written or broadcast material which should not be ignored. There are signs of a new willingness by police and the CPS to use these laws more vigorously and imaginatively. The Home Office is also improving its efforts to monitor their use to curb racist activity. This gives some encouragement to those who complain of racist abuse and harassment to report it to the police.

SECTION 2

POSITION POST-HRA

The rights which most affect the law concerning freedom of expression and hate speech are those in Articles 6, 8, 9, and 10.

Article 6

Right to a Fair Trial

Article 6 protects the right to a fair and public hearing wherever a person's civil rights or any criminal charge are determined. This could mean that a person who claims to be the victim of racial abuse or harassment can insist on a proper hearing before a court.

This is in fact provided already in many cases by the statutes described earlier, but there could still be cases where a right to be free from racism in some form is claimed, yet no opportunity is provided under existing law for the matter to be adjudicated by a court. An example is provided by the case of *Osman* ([1999] EHRLR 251). This decided that the immunity traditionally claimed by the police and other public authorities from legal action for negligence in carrying out their operational duties was a violation of Article 6. Hence failure by the police to investigate allegations of racial harassment, though not actionable hitherto by domestic law, may now be challenged as a breach of the HRA.

Article 8

Right to Respect for Private and Family Life

Paradoxically, Article 8 – guaranteeing respect for private and family life, home and correspondence – could provide an argument in defence of a charge of possessing racially inflammatory material under the POA. However, Article 8 permits interference in accordance with the law with the exercise of the right, where it is necessary in a democratic society for the protection of the rights and freedoms of others. This is likely to justify what might otherwise be a violation of Article 8 in order to combat racism or racial incitement.

Article 9

Freedom of Thought, Conscience and Religion

Article 9, protecting the right to freedom of thought, conscience and religion, may well protect the right to hold racist opinions, and private religious observance where racist beliefs are part and parcel of a particular creed, for example where a particular sect has restricted its membership on a racial basis.

However, the public expression of racist views, amounting to racial incitement, under the guise of religious expression or worship, could raise difficult issues under the HRA. Article 9 contains a similar qualification to that in Article 8 permitting limitations on the right where prescribed by law and necessary in a democratic society for the protection of the rights and freedoms of others, but s.13 HRA requires any court or tribunal to have particular regard to the importance of the right to freedom of thought, conscience and religion when deciding any question which might affect the exercise of that right by a religious organisation. The expression of racist religious views might thus be difficult to challenge successfully by legal action.

Article 10

Freedom of expression

Article 10 is the most important provision of the Convention in relation to racial incitement and hate speech.

While it states the important principle of freedom of expression and its purpose is to protect speech and expression of any kind, it is also subject to the limitation that interference with it can be justified where necessary in a democratic society to protect the rights and freedoms of others. Restrictions imposed by law on racist speech which amounts to harassment or incitement, as in the statutory provisions outlined above, are therefore likely to fall within the class of permitted restrictions and any attempt to rely on Article 10 to defend racist speech is likely to fail.

However, in *Jersild v Denmark* [1994] 19 EHRR 1, the ECtHR said that the reporting by journalists of racially inflammatory statements made by others should not be restricted in a democratic society unless the purpose of such reporting was the propagation of racist views and ideas. In other words, merely carrying out the responsibility of a journalist to inform the public of the dangerous activities of racists should not be penalised. On the contrary, it can be argued that journalists who alert the public to the dangers of racism, even where this involves incidentally describing or publicising their activities, are performing a valuable public service in a mature society.

The protection of freedom of expression for journalists who report objectively the activities of racists is very different from protecting the activities of racists themselves, who are unlikely to gain any protection or comfort by relying on Article 10.

Article 10 will of course protect anti-racist expression and any attempt (however unlikely that may be) to curb or restrict the publication of anti-racist literature or campaigning material would be open to challenge. Reference has already been made to the law of defamation as a valid restriction on freedom of expression. Proceedings for defamation or libel will continue to be a risk that anti-racist publications will always have to keep in mind where individuals or commercial organisations are accused of racism. Care must always be taken to avoid such accusations unless the facts can be established to justify them.

SECTION 3
WHO CAN CLAIM?

As is generally the case under the HRA only the victim of a violation can successfully claim. Others who may be affected by the violation, such as a spouse who may suffer distress as a result of racial harassment or incitement of his or her partner, have no claim under the HRA. Similarly, it does not appear to be open to an organisation representing victims to pursue a claim in its own name, though it may assist the victim or victims to claim in their own names, for example through the provision of funding to meet legal fees.

SECTION 4

WHO IS LIABLE?

Liability under the HRA is restricted to public authorities and others only to the extent that they are engaged in public functions. An authority will however be liable for violations committed by its employees within the scope of their employment and in some circumstances by agents acting on behalf of the authority. It should be noted that public authorities include the Government itself and the courts but do not include Parliament or a person exercising functions in connection with proceedings in Parliament.

SECTION 5

Case Study
Consider the following circumstances.

A well-known racist writer, NF, publishes a novel describing the murderous activities of the Ku Klux Klan in the southern United States. The leaders of this organisation are presented as heroes performing a public service and the clear message is conveyed that a similar criminal movement would be welcome in Britain. NF is prosecuted for incitement to racial hatred. NF defends himself by claiming that the prosecution violates his right to freedom of expression under Article 10. He invites the High Court to declare that the relevant provisions of the Public Order Act are incompatible with the Convention.

What will the court do? Pay particular regard to:

- The proviso in paragraph 2 of Article 10, allowing restrictions to be placed on the right to freedom of expression for the protection of the rights and freedoms of others and for the prevention of disorder or crime.
- Article 4(a) of the International Convention on the Elimination of All Forms of Discrimination. This requires the States that are parties to it (including the United Kingdom) 'to declare as an offence punishable by law ... incitement to racial discrimination, as well as all acts of violence or incitement to such acts against any race or group of persons of another colour or ethnic origin'.

Religious discrimination

Makbool Javaid

This chapter examines the role played by the HRA in combating religious discrimination, primarily in the employment field.

SECTION 1

POSITION PRE-HRA

The connections between race and religion

In the RRA, 'racial group' means a group of persons defined by reference to colour, race, nationality or ethnic or national origins – but not religious belief. Yet racial origins and religion are closely intertwined. Ethnic minority groups coming to this country have often brought with them, as part of their identity, distinctive religions and religious practices. Many members of these communities see themselves as proud inheritors of major world civilisations. Moreover, faced with prejudice and discrimination on the part of the majority community, many members of the ethnic minority communities respond by emphasising their distinctive religious and cultural identities.

No specific religious discrimination law

At present, in England, Wales and Scotland, discrimination on grounds of religion is not unlawful. In Northern Ireland, however, the Fair Employment Acts offer protection against discrimination and make it unlawful to discriminate on religious grounds in employment. By the Fair Employment and Treatment (Northern Ireland) Order 1998, this protection also covers further and higher education and the provision of goods, facilities and services.

Despite the present absence of specific protection, however, the RRA has been used to prevent discrimination against some religious groups and consequently, in a limited way, has protected against religious discrimination. As explained in the Introduction, the RRA makes reference to 'direct' and 'indirect' discrimination. It is important to understand the implications of both forms of discrimination in order to appreciate how the protections offered by the RRA may be used in the context of religious discrimination.

The EC has recently agreed a new directive, the Employment Framework Directive, which obliges the UK Government to provide protection from discrimination on grounds of religion and belief by at least December 2003. In October 2002, the DTI issued for consultation the draft Employment Equality (Religion or Belief) Regulations 2003, which purport to implement the Directive. When in force, these Regulations will change much of what follows. Importantly, however, this will only be in the employment context.

How to challenge religious discrimination

By using concepts of discrimination under the RRA, discrimination on grounds of religion has been successfully challenged. This will continue to be an effective avenue to pursue either in itself or, more importantly in the context of this chapter, in conjunction with a claim under the HRA.

Presently under the RRA, there are two situations where discrimination on the grounds of religion might be successfully claimed: where the religious group itself falls within the protection of the RRA as a racial group; or where the religious group is dominant in either one or more racial groups. The first claim is, broadly speaking, a claim for direct discrimination. The latter is one of indirect discrimination.

Religious discrimination as direct racial discrimination

The RRA defines racial discrimination as including discrimination on grounds of a person's membership of a group defined by reference to its 'ethnic origin'. Consequently, religious groups that can also bring themselves within the definition of an ethnic group can obtain the protection of the RRA. The courts are willing to consider that a group of individuals may amount to an 'ethnic group' for the purposes of the RRA if the group regards itself as being (and, in turn, the group is regarded by others as being) a distinct community by virtue of certain characteristics, two of which are essential. These are:

- A long shared history, of which the group was conscious, as distinguishing it from other groups; and
- A cultural tradition of its own, including family and social customs and manners – often, although not necessarily, associated with religious observance.

In addition, the following characteristics are relevant:

- Either a common geographical origin or descent from a small number of common ancestors;

- A common language, which did not necessarily have to be peculiar to the group;
- A common literature peculiar to the group;
- A common religion different from that of neighbouring groups;
- The characteristic of being a minority or being an oppressed or a dominant group within a larger community.

Individuals can fall into a particular racial group either by birth or by adopting and following the customs of the group ('conversion'), provided that they consider themselves to be a member of the group and are accepted by others as such.

Applying the above approach, the courts have ruled that Sikhs and Jews are both distinct ethnic groups and therefore are entitled to the protection of the RRA. Consequently, a discriminatory act against a Sikh may be challenged as amounting to direct discrimination under the RRA, notwithstanding that the discrimination itself may be based more on the person's religion. However, where applying the RRA in the case of Jews, it is important to distinguish between Jews as being a racial group (in which case any less favourable treatment will amount to direct discrimination) and religious observance by Jews (when the discrimination is likely to be indirect).

The courts have in the past held that Muslims, Rastafarians and members of the Seventh Day Adventist Church do not amount to racial groups for the purposes of the RRA. It is unlikely that other religious groups will be able to demonstrate that they are entitled to the protection of the RRA since they will be unlikely to demonstrate that they are able to satisfy the requirement that they possess the characteristics of an ethnic group.

Religious discrimination as indirect racial discrimination

There are instances where religious or cultural characteristics may coincide with racial characteristics. In such situations it is sometimes possible to argue that an act of religious discrimination in effect amounts to unlawful indirect discrimination against a particular racial group. For example, discrimination against Muslims or Hindus may, in certain circumstances, constitute indirect racial discrimination against Pakistanis, Bangladeshis or Indians. There have been several cases where individuals who have suffered discrimination on account of their religion have been able to prove that such discrimination constituted unlawful indirect racial discrimination under the terms of the RRA.

Unlawful indirect racial discrimination has been successfully argued in a variety of situations:

- Dress codes and uniform requirements (for example, where female employees have been precluded from wearing trousers and/or nose

studs; where men have been prevented from wearing turbans);
- Refusal to allow time off for daily worship (for example, to attend prayers during work time, or being prevented from taking a longer lunch break on Friday or to observe the Sabbath);
- Refusal to allow employees to observe religious holidays;
- Rules on facial hair (precluding men from wearing beards);
- Refusal to employ individuals from certain religious groups;
- A requirement for a food technologist to taste non-Kosher food.

In considering whether a particular rule or practice of an employer will potentially amount to indirect discrimination under the RRA, it is important to bear in mind the following.

Indirect discrimination is concerned with a rule or practice, whether or not such practice is in writing, which has the effect of disadvantaging certain racial groups. It is not necessary for an employee to demonstrate that such a rule is expressly stated in their written job description or contract of employment. Although it might be difficult to prove, it is sufficient that the employee can illustrate that such a rule is in existence by explaining what the employer in practice requires.

At the moment it is still necessary to show that the rule being challenged is an absolute bar. If an employer argues that a particular rule is only a preference or something they consider to be desirable, it is not possible to challenge it. Nevertheless, if in reality all employees are required to comply with the rule then it would be possible to argue that although the employer argues that it is merely a preference on their part, it in actual fact amounts to an absolute barrier.

It is not always necessary to produce detailed statistics to show that fewer people from a racial group can comply with the practice. However, statistical information, which can be obtained from the Commission for Racial Equality, Racial Equality Councils, Local Authorities and Annual Labour Force Surveys may assist in demonstrating that discrimination has taken place. If relying on such information, a party is advised to arrange for a suitable witness to attend the Employment Tribunal, although it might well accept written evidence in the form of a letter from such organisations. On the other hand, a tribunal might be persuaded to take account of the obvious, for example a 'no beard' rule will affect certain racial groups more than others, for example Jews, Sikhs and those in which Muslims are predominant.

An individual can belong to more than one racial group. For example, in order to create the most favourable statistical picture a Muslim could either be non-white, Asian, Arab, Pakistani or Indian (those racial groups in which Islam is the dominant faith).

Remember that, although the employee may physically be able to comply with a rule, the issue is whether compliance will require the individual to breach a religious requirement. To establish whether this might apply, it may be necessary to ask an expert witness to testify, for example a priest, academic or community representative. Such an expert will be required to establish his/her expertise to the tribunal.

New Directives

The EC has agreed two new Directives.

The first is the Race Directive whose purpose is to establish in all Member States the principle of equal treatment between individuals irrespective of their racial or ethnic origin. It has a wide scope and applies not only to employment and working conditions but also to social protection and social security, education and access to and supply of goods and services. The UK government must implement this directive into UK law by at least July 2003.

The second is the Employment Framework Directive. As stated above, this will provide protection from discrimination on grounds of religion or belief in the field of employment and working conditions. These are widely defined and will include not only employment conditions but also terms for self-employment, vocational training and membership of professional organisations. It is likely that the definition of religion or belief will also be widely defined in line with Article 9 (see below). The UK Government will have to incorporate this into UK law by at least December 2003 and draft Regulations have already been issued

SECTION 2

POSITION POST-HRA

The ECtHR has declared that freedom of religion is one of 'the foundations of a pluralistic and democratic society'. It will be interesting to see whether this view is borne out in practice with the application of the HRA.

Article 9

Freedom of Thought, Conscience and Religion

Article 9 guarantees the right to freedom of thought, conscience and religion; freedom to change religion or belief; and, either alone or in the community with others, and in public or in private, to manifest religion or belief, in worship, teaching, practice and observance.

Article 9 represents a substantial change to English law. As explained above, prior to the implementation of the HRA, a religious discrimination claim was dependent upon establishing that racial discrimination had taken place. Although the RRA will continue to be an important method of challenging religious discrimination, the HRA allows individuals to raise fresh arguments and, wherever possible, combine them with RRA claims.

No need to define religion
Under the RRA (see above), the courts have had to define the meaning of 'racial group'. Under the HRA there is probably little need to make a definitive ruling on what constitutes a religion since the wording of Article 9 has been widely interpreted to include all the major world religions as well as the Krishna Consciousness movement, the Church of Scientology, Druidism, pacifism and veganism. It also covers atheists and agnostics. There is a limit to this in that the belief system must have a serious ideology having some cogency or coherence. It does not extend to political views.

Absolute right to belief
It is important to note that the right to belief, described as the 'inner' character of religious faith or conscience, is absolute and cannot be interfered with under any circumstances. An individual relying on Article 9 will have to demonstrate that he or she adheres to a particular belief or practice. It will not be necessary to show how strongly the belief is held but there will be a need to indicate how the manifestation being curtailed is required by, or accords with, the individual's belief or religion.

Manifestation of belief
In the context of employment, the most significant issues will relate to the manifestation of religion or belief and any restrictions that are imposed. The general principle that will need to borne in mind is whether the act under consideration is motivated by the employee's belief or simply incidental to it. If the religious observance is a voluntary or permissible act, as opposed to one that is compulsory, the employer might be able to argue that there is no breach if this is denied to the employee.

For example, the use of Henna as body art on face and hands at weddings is a cultural, not a religious requirement, and consequently an employer might refuse to allow employees to attend work having participated in such a ritual. However, a refusal might amount to a breach of the freedom of expression; see Article 10.

It is likely that the courts will view established religions more sympathetically than manifestations of faith motivated by unfamiliar or secular beliefs.

Justification of interference with religious freedom
The questions to consider here involve:

- To what extent did the employer recognise the employee's religious views or beliefs?
- Those relating to the nature of the employer's defence: for example, did the employer's policy amount to a mere inconvenience for the employee or could it be viewed as a significant curtailment of religious practice?
- To what extent was the employee aware of the potential for working practices to interfere with his or her beliefs before taking on the job? Were any terms or conditions of the contract of employment drawn to his or her attention at the start of employment?
- What has been the impact of the employee's religious observance on the freedom of religion of other employees? For example, is there improper proselytising on the part of the employee?

Read in conjunction with Articles 10 and 14, the kinds of issues that may now be challenged could include:

- Rules relating to appearance (the use of Henna, tattoos or body paint);
- A refusal to work on certain days of the week. Presently Jewish employees have difficulty in arguing indirect racial discrimination, as the figures indicate that only a small minority of Jews observe the Sabbath. Under the HRA, however, this will not be a problem. Similarly, Seventh Day Adventists have had very little chance of establishing indirect racial discrimination, whereas under the HRA they will be able to demonstrate that the importance of their religious beliefs is common to their Church and a fundamental part of their belief;
- A refusal to perform certain tasks which might be incidental to the job for which the individual has been hired (for example, attending client lunches where alcohol is served may be offensive to a Muslim. Similarly, the serving of non-Kosher food might be offensive to a Jew);
- A refusal to be alone with a member of the opposite sex (for example, requiring an employee to share a room or go on a overnight trip);
- A refusal to shake hands with someone of the opposite sex;
- A demand for the employer to provide facilities for ablution and prayers at work;
- A refusal by a female Muslim to allow an identification photograph to be taken without her head being covered;
- A ban on religious propaganda such as leaflets, cassettes, videos at work, the use of e-mail to post notices of religious events or pass on greetings;

- A ban on religious meetings, discussion groups and celebrations;
- A refusal to allow employees to fast because of work commitments or health and safety reasons;
- A refusal to take back a Muslim employee returning to work after pilgrimage with a shaved head, or accepting a Rastafarian with dreadlocks;
- Smoking or possession of marijuana at work by a Rastafarian.

It is more than likely that the most effective use of Article 9 will be as an adjunct to an indirect racial discrimination claim rather than as a freestanding challenge (see the chapter on employment for a more detailed discussion of this). However, the HRA will for the first time allow individuals from racial groups that are not identified with particular religions to bring claims. Under the HRA, we may see white or Afro-Caribbean British citizens who convert to Hinduism or the Krishna Consciousness Movement bringing claims. Rastafarians who comprise only a minority within their 'racial' or 'national' group will for the first time be able to be bring effective challenges to practices that interfere with their religious beliefs.

Article 14

Prohibition of Discrimination

The point has been made elsewhere that Article 14 is not a freestanding right. In this context, obviously it would be used most commonly in conjunction with Article 9 (although some issues such as the right to wear religiously dictated dress could raise issues under Articles 8 and 10).

The proposed new Protocol 12 would remedy this deficiency as if adopted it will provide for a freestanding equality right.

Not every distinction or difference in treatment will be regarded as unlawful discrimination under Article 14. The ECtHR has held that differential treatment may be permitted where there is a reasonable and objective justification, where the differential treatment is in pursuit of a legitimate aim, and where there is proportionality between the effects of the measures and the objectives.

SECTION 3

WHO CAN CLAIM?

In terms of determining the types of employees and employers who may bring these types of HRA-influenced claims, readers should cross-refer to the employment chapter.

SECTION 4

WHO IS LIABLE?

Again, there is a more detailed discussion of this in the employment chapter.

SECTION 5

Case Study

A Local Authority's employees are contractually required to work on Saturday and Sunday shifts. Otherwise, there is a general 37 hours Monday to Friday working week. After he has been working with the Local Authority for a few weeks, an employee, Ahmed, asks for time off on Fridays to attend prayers at the nearest mosque. He is refused. He claims that the Local Authority is acting in breach of the Convention.

Which right (or rights) are involved? Is he correct? What about employees who regard Saturdays and Sundays as holy days?

Ahmed may have a case against the Local Authority for indirect discrimination contrary to the RRA as the policy may impact disproportionately on individuals originating from the Indian Sub-Continent who are adherents of Islam.

A similar situation to this arose in *Ahmed v UK*. It was decided that there was no right to interference with the right to freedom of religion under Article 9. The right to manifest religion and to engage in religious worship is a qualified right under Article 9. Mr Ahmed had accepted his job that required him to work on Fridays, without stipulating that he would need time off for worship, and his rights under Article 9 would have to be balanced against his professional obligations. Furthermore it was found that Mr Ahmed had not been discriminated against in breach of Article 14 in conjunction with Article 9. Mr Ahmed did not receive less favourable treatment than employees who were members of other religious groups, and it was acceptable that public holidays should reflect the religions of the majority of the population.

Social welfare law

Stephen Simblet

The HRA is having a number of important effects in social welfare law. The impact of the HRA is fairly predictable in the mental health area, but is more speculative insofar as entitlement to services is concerned.

SECTION 1
POSITION PRE-HRA

What is social welfare law?
This is the law concerning the allocation of resources to individuals to provide for their needs. The principal source of this sort of law is statutory, and provides a range of duties and discretions for determining an individual's entitlement. The statutory system will generally set out a regime for assessing needs and then, depending on the outcome of that assessment, it will set out a duty to pay a particular benefit or a duty or discretion to provide a particular service.

With this area of law, it is almost always going to be the case that the individual's opponent will be a public body, whether that be a local authority, a social security adjudication officer and so on. This will be important when we come to consider the applicability of the HRA in Section 2.

Current institutions and procedures
Where a dispute arises, there is very often a means of resolving that dispute through a tribunal specific to that particular legislation, such as the Social Security Appeals Tribunal. In cases where there is no means of appealing against such a decision, or where all of the rights of appeal have been exhausted, there may be recourse to the courts, either by exercising a statutory right of appeal to the Court of Appeal or by way of judicial review.

Judicial review, in particular, is a very restricted remedy. The Court cannot re-take the decision that is challenged. The most it can do is to 'quash' the decision or require that it be re-taken lawfully. Also, the remedy only exists where the court can say that a public body has acted outside its powers, by making an error of law, acting unfairly, or acting in a way in which no reasonable body could act. This is known as 'Wednesbury unreasonableness'. Even if such an error can be established, the court may not quash the decision challenged. Also, and importantly, judicial review is not available where the person complaining has some other remedy, for example an appeal to a tribunal.

Prior to the HRA coming into force, there was no right to obtain compensation from the courts for errors made by public bodies in the exercise of the sort of statutory functions discussed above. The reasons why are extremely complicated, and beyond the scope of this book. This will probably change now that the HRA is in force.

Since the coming into force of the RR(A)A, public bodies are prohibited from discriminating on racial grounds in the carrying out of any of their functions. The amended RRA now applies to aspects of social welfare such as the use of coercive powers under the laws relating to mental health or child protection, and rights of redress are available where racial discrimination occurs.

It would also be unlawful and 'Wednesbury' unreasonable for a decision-taker to act in a manner that deliberately discriminated on grounds of race. Even at the time of the Wednesbury case, one of the examples of unreasonable conduct was a decision to deny a benefit on the grounds that the recipient had red hair. However, the problems that arise in the social welfare field and the supply of services do not normally lead to *deliberate* denial of service on racial grounds. What is more likely is that the public body's policies and procedures have a discriminatory *effect*.

Pre-HRA difficulties

One of the problems that often used to occur in relation to racial discrimination was where the decision-taker's decision, while not actually motivated by considerations of race, had the effect of unlawfully discriminating. An example from the community care context is this: a local authority offers to move a family with a disabled child into a ground-floor property, but has a practice or policy that it will only provide a two-bedroom property in such cases. Such a policy would be likely to discriminate against Asian children, who tend to live in larger families. While in certain circumstances the policy would be unlawful, it is by no means certain that it could be successfully challenged in judicial review proceedings. Considerations of resources, other services and other sources of help might all be factored into the decision such that, ultimately, the council's policy would not be held to be unreasonable.

The possibility for legal action to combat racial discrimination in social welfare provision is greater since the RR(A)A imposed the new general duties on public bodies discussed in Chapter 2. These duties require public bodies to have due regard to the elimination of unlawful discrimination and the promotion of equality of opportunity and good race relations when carrying out their policies and functions. Failure to do so could be challenged by way of judicial review. Public authorities involved in social welfare provision also have specific duties under the Home Secretary's order (see Chapter 2, above), including a duty to have arrangements for assessing the race equality impact of new policies before they are adopted. The CRE has enforcement powers in relation to these specific duties.

Another example concerns procedures in social security tribunals, for instance on an adjudication of a claim for incapacity benefit and the 'all work' test. The tribunal is inquisitorial in nature, meaning that it is required to find the facts for itself, assisted by the claimant and any representations by the DSS made through a presenting officer. Under the current social security legislation, the Secretary of State makes the appointment of members of the tribunal. The tribunal need not consider an issue that has not been raised on the face of the appeal (s.12(8)(a) SSA). An appellant in the tribunal is unable to have professional assistance through the Legal Aid scheme. Since he or she is in receipt of benefit, it is unlikely that they could afford to pay for legal representation. If the appellant failed to put material details about his or her medical condition in the grounds of appeal to the tribunal, the tribunal could lawfully refuse to consider the material. In cases where the Appellant did not speak very good English and/or had filled in the form alone, it would be very easy for an important detail to be omitted.

If the Tribunal refused to allow the point to be considered, such a refusal *might* be susceptible to challenge on appeal or by judicial review, but the merits of the matter not inquired into might never be investigated. It would only be if the decision taken were perverse that judicial review would afford a remedy. In this rather complex way, it can be seen that, before the HRA, a process with a racially discriminatory effect may actually have been lawful.

SECTION 2

POSITION POST-HRA

Some of the important changes in the social welfare context have been the changes introduced by the RR(A)A, and changes made to judicial review. On applications for judicial review, the test of 'Wednesbury' unreasonableness is disappearing: a new ground of illegality has been introduced by the HRA, in that it is unlawful for a public authority to act in a way that is incompatible with a Convention right. The HRA has, however, already introduced an important reform to the Wednesbury test, where the conduct being challenged affects human rights. The decision of the House of Lords in *Queen on application of Daly v Secretary of State for Home Department* [2001] 2 WLR 1622 was that the court is obliged to consider the proportionality of executive action which interferes with fundamental human rights and that disproportionate interference is unlawful.

The Rights under the Convention that are of particular significance in this context are Articles 3, 6, 8 and 14.

Article 3

Prohibition of Torture

It is unlikely that it was contemplated when the Convention was drafted that inhuman or degrading treatment may extend into such things as the condition of very ill people and the provision of services. For instance, there might be a situation in which a person claiming a community care service is suffering from chronic conditions which, if not alleviated, would result in continuation of a very unpleasant medical condition, which might be regarded as inhuman or degrading treatment.

There are some cases from the Strasbourg Court in which prisoners (i.e. those who are unable by reasons of detention to care for themselves) have been held to be subject to inhuman and degrading treatment in similar circumstances. To take the facts of one case, a prisoner who had soiled his trousers was not able to change them for one day. This was held to be inhuman treatment: *Hurtado v Switzerland* [1994] A 280A. Further, a decision to deport a person suffering from AIDS to a country in which there was no proper treatment or care for sufferers from that condition has been found to amount to inhuman treatment: *D v UK* [1997] 1 EHRR 423. It might therefore be open to argue, in sufficiently extreme cases, that a particular medical condition (even though the state has not caused it) needs to be ameliorated. A withdrawal of service provision, for example, might amount to inhuman or degrading treatment in particular circumstances.

There are some illnesses, such as AIDS, that appear in a much greater density in some populations and racial groups than others. It might be possible to contest particular biasing of service provision, to the detriment of such people, on these grounds. In other cases of racial discrimination, the ECtHR has held that deliberate racial discrimination and harassment, at the level applied by the Idi Amin regime to Ugandan Asians, amounts to a breach of Article 3: *East African Asians Case* [1973] 13 EHRR 76.

It is worth observing that Article 3 is an 'unqualified' right. In simple terms, there is either a breach of the right or there is not. Unlike with many other Articles, there is no room for discussion as to the purposes for which there has been an interference with the right.

Article 5

The Right to Liberty and Security of the Person

The first 'declaration of incompatibility' under the HRA was made in relation to the burden of proof applied in the Mental Health Review Tribunal, in a case called *Queen on application of H v Mental Health Review Tribunal* [2001] 3 WLR 512. Further, the speediness of access to the Mental Health Review Tribunal, which is the only mechanism for challenging detention under the Mental Health Act 1983, was significantly affected by the decision in *Queen on application of C v Mental Health Review Tribunal* [2001] 4 CCLR 284.

Article 6

Right to a Fair Trial

A great deal of the social security system, including complaints procedures for community care services, comprises some form of adjudication. There are a number of decisions by the ECtHR to the effect that social security benefits are civil rights, and thus fall within Article 6. There are a number of fairly obvious biases in the current system, as outlined above. The appointments procedure may deny the applicant a fair trial of his or her appeal. Furthermore, the inequality of knowledge between a claimant (particularly a claimant whose first language is not English) and the DSS presenting officer may mean there may not be fair adjudication.

Article 8

Right to Respect for Private and Family Life

Article 8 rights are well worth considering when considering the adequacy of service provision in the community care context. Article 8 is a qualified right, in that some interference is permissible. Article 8 encompasses far more than just a right to be left alone. There are a number of cases, including the recent unsuccessful application by a disabled man concerning disability access at a public beach (*Botta v Italy* [1999] CCLR), in which the ECtHR has made plain that Article 8 has a dimension of substantive entitlements.

If one returns to the example of a local authority failing to provide a ground-floor flat to a disabled Asian child, it may no longer be sufficient for the authority just to say that it does not have any accommodation. The effect of denying the transfer to a ground floor flat may be that the child is unable to continue to live with his or her parents.

On a challenge by way of judicial review, the Court would have to consider whether or not there has been an interference with the child's rights (and the parents' rights) to family life. It is likely that such interference would be found. The Court would then have to consider whether or not the interference was in accordance with law and necessary for any of the reasons contained in Article 8(2). At this point, fairly detailed evidence of needs could be submitted, and the court's inquiry, in addressing the issue of proportionality, would be of much wider scope than was the position in pre-HRA judicial review cases. Such detailed evidence is likely to include statistics on need, on family size among the Asian community and so on. The Court would have to include all of this in its discussions on need.

Another example would concern a withdrawal of service provision. If an elderly service user had her meals on wheels withdrawn, and she was unable to cook, it might feasibly be contended in extreme cases that this was inhuman or degrading treatment, although the possibility of moving elsewhere to a catered home would probably mean that no breach of Article 3 could be established. However, such a move could more realistically mean that there is interference with the right to privacy, family life and respect for the home. In considering the test of proportionality, the substantive merits of this decision would have to be set against the effect on the service user and the numbers affected.

Such an inquiry would go far outside the current parameters of pre-HRA judicial review. And a pro-active caseworker, who might have a number of similar cases and be networked to a number of organisations, may be able to collate this sort of evidence in a skilful and imaginative way.

Article 14

Prohibition of Discrimination
If breaches of Articles 3, 6 or 8 can be shown in the manner described above, it may not always be necessary to invoke Article 14. However, in cases involving a racially discriminatory aspect of treatment, reference may also need to be made to the provisions of Article 14.

SECTION 3
WHO CAN CLAIM?

Anyone who is a 'victim' under the HRA can claim under the HRA. In the context of social welfare law, it is likely that almost everyone who would, as a private individual, have sufficient standing to bring a claim for judicial review, will fall under the HRA.

SECTION 4

WHO IS LIABLE?

In the social welfare context, decisions taken are by local authorities and other statutory bodies, which will certainly fulfil the definition of public authorities in s.6 HRA.

SECTION 5

Case Study

Mr X comes from Rwanda. He has a number of mental health problems. He has been detained in hospital in the past. He does not have any family in this country, and his social work team are concerned about his level of isolation. In the view of his psychiatrist, one of the features of his mental illness and one of the factors that triggers it, is the fact that he can get disoriented. It is thought that he ought to have a placement at a day-care centre in which he will be surrounded by other African staff and service users. This features in an assessment of his community care needs. However, the local authority that is responsible for providing services says that such a placement is impractical and too costly.

If you are asked to assist Mr X, what potential issues would you need to consider, in order to try and achieve a suitable placement?

1. *What remedies would lie, prior to the HRA?*
   Aside from exploring the complaints procedure, there might be an application for judicial review of the failure to provide adequate services, but this would be unlikely to succeed, since the decision and the basis for it were within the powers of the local authority and had a rational basis.

2. *Is the local authority a public authority?*
   Yes: there is no doubt.

3. *What other arguments are there, after the HRA?*
   Mr X's Article 8 rights are engaged here, and there is a great deal of case-law to the effect that Article 8 is about one's identity and the

substantive entitlement to respect for that identity. It may no longer be sufficient for the decision merely to be rational. Also, is there a question of discrimination on grounds either of national origins or race? The key question is the reality of service-provision. There may be an easily attainable way of achieving the access to persons who share Mr X's culture, and simply asserting that there is no such placement is not an adequate response.

4. *Who should be contacted?*
    The local authority social work department should be reminded of their responsibilities to provide those services required by the assessment.

5. *Will public funding be available?*
    Almost certainly.

Racial harassment outside the workplace

Rajiv Menon

This chapter examines the role that the HRA plays in combating racial harassment outside the workplace. The term 'racial harassment' is being used in the broad sense to encompass the full range of racially motivated crime including abuse, harassment and violence.

SECTION 1

POSITION PRE-HRA

Police powers to combat racial harassment

The police response to racial harassment has been the subject of sustained criticism for many years. The Stephen Lawrence Inquiry report published in 1999 merely confirmed what ethnic minority communities and civil liberties organisations had been saying for years about institutional racism within the police service. However, it is essential to note that the problem has never been about the failure of domestic criminal law to provide the police with sufficient powers to tackle racial harassment. Indeed, even prior to the introduction of racially aggravated offences in 1998, there was no shortage of possible criminal charges that could be brought against those engaging in racial harassment. The problem has consistently been about the failure of the police to use those powers available under domestic law to combat racial harassment properly and effectively.

A detailed analysis of the police powers to arrest, detain and search is beyond the scope of this chapter. What is important to know is that, under PACE, an officer may arrest without warrant anyone who he or she reasonably suspects of having committed or being about to commit most relevant criminal offences. In addition, under common law, an officer may arrest without warrant anyone who he or she reasonably suspects of having committed or being about to commit a breach of the peace. In short, the power to arrest perpetrators of racial harassment arises in almost any conceivable situation where racial harassment is reported to the police.

Depending on the nature of the racial harassment, a perpetrator could be arrested for and charged with one or more of the following criminal offences:

- An offence against the person – including murder, wounding, causing grievous bodily harm, assault occasioning actual bodily harm and common assault;
- A public order offence – including affray, threatening behaviour, disorderly behaviour and inciting racial hatred;
- An offence of criminal damage;
- An offence of harassment;
- An offence of possessing an offensive weapon or having a bladed/pointed article in a public place;
- A racially aggravated offence of assault, public order, criminal damage or harassment.

Ultimately, the police response to racial harassment will be judged by the number of perpetrators of racial harassment being arrested and charged and the extent that they are being charged with offences that properly reflect the criminality inherent in their actions.

Having said that, sometimes there are good reasons not to arrest an identified perpetrator of racial harassment (for example, if the victim is adamant that he or she does not want an arrest to be made). Very occasionally, the perpetrator is unknown and difficult to identify. Even in such cases, there are obvious elementary steps that the police can take to investigate the complaint, prevent further harassment and generally improve their response. If there is an identified perpetrator, the police can warn him or her about the consequences of further harassment. In all cases, the police can re-assure the victim that the complaint is being taken seriously and will be properly investigated.

In short, there is tremendous scope under domestic criminal law to put pressure on the police and the CPS to criminalise racial harassment. This should be the foundation upon which any reliance on the HRA is built.

Other statutory powers to combat racial harassment
Whilst the police service has the primary frontline responsibility for ensuring that racial harassment is tackled seriously by the state, other public

authorities have duties and responsibilities as well. For example, local authorities, state schools and NHS trusts all have a role to play in improving race relations, combating racial harassment and ensuring that the services they provide are not racially discriminatory in any way.

Many local authorities now have policies designed to protect the right of council tenants (and in some cases even the right of those living in the private sector) to live free of racial attack. Some local authorities have evicted council tenants who have engaged in persistent racial harassment and obtained civil injunctions to prevent further harassment.

As with the police, there is great scope to pressure other public authorities to introduce policies tackling racial harassment and to ensure that those policies have real teeth and are properly implemented and monitored.

Effect of the RR(A)A
The RR(A)A brought the police, the CPS and all other public authorities within the scope of the RRA. Thus there must be no racial discrimination in, for example, making arrests, deciding whom to prosecute, managing council housing or using local authority powers to prevent harassment. The RR(A)A also imposes a positive duty on the police, local authorities, schools, NHS trusts and other public bodies to eliminate discrimination (including harassment) and to promote good race relations in carrying out their various functions. These bodies must monitor how their policies impact on race equality and publish the results of this monitoring.

Racial harassment by the police or other public authorities
If the racial harassment alleged is by an employee of the police or other public authority, then the victim has the right to take proceedings in the Employment Tribunal (see the chapter on Employment Law) and/or to make an official complaint.

Where the victim of racial harassment is a member of the public then, under the amended RRA, he or she can sue the police or other public body in the County Court, as the RRA makes them liable for the acts of racial harassment by their employees. In addition, depending on the nature of the racial harassment, a public authority could be liable for the following torts of its employees:

- Assault and battery
- False imprisonment
- Malicious prosecution
- Misfeasance in public office
- Breach of statutory duty

- Negligence
- Trespass to land
- Wrongful interference with goods.

SECTION 2

POSITION POST-HRA

The HRA introduces constitutional rights whose primary role is to strengthen and not replace existing rights under domestic law. In certain situations, individuals can raise fresh arguments relying on Convention precedents, often combining them with existing arguments under domestic law. It is hoped that that the creation of a rights-based culture in the years ahead will fundamentally improve the access that citizens have to the law and the courts.

There are two schools of thought on whether and to what extent the HRA is directly effective against private parties. One school argues that the HRA is aimed entirely at disputes between the individual and the state rather than at disputes between private parties. The other school argues that the courts being public authorities must act in accordance with Convention rights and that any distinction between the public and the private is, therefore, artificial.

In reality, one private party cannot sue another for breach of a Convention right. Private parties can, however, sue public authorities (including the courts) for acting in a manner incompatible with Convention rights or perhaps even for failing to protect private parties from having their Convention rights violated by other private parties.

Consequently, the HRA does not directly assist in the prosecution of perpetrators of racial harassment. However, if the police or another public authority fails to take appropriate preventative action against perpetrators of racial harassment, then there might be a cause of action against the public authority under the HRA.

It is important to remember that the Convention is 'designed to maintain and promote the ideals and values of a democratic society' including 'pluralism, tolerance and broad-mindedness' (see *Kjeldsen v Denmark* (1976) 1 EHRR 711 and *Handyside v UK* (1976) 1 EHRR 737).

A word of caution: whilst the incorporation of the Convention may provide many new and exciting avenues for legal challenge, it only provides certain *minimum* rights that do not always offer more protection than existing rights under domestic common law. For example, it does not protect many social and economic rights that we often take for granted and it is plainly not a panacea for all complaints. Consequently, while it should be used where it assists, we should not become over-reliant upon it.

Article 2

Right to Life

Article 2 places a positive duty on the state to protect and safeguard life. It is arguable that the state has breached Article 2 if:

- There was a risk to the life of a private individual from the actual or threatened criminal acts of a third party;
- The risk was real and immediate;
- A public authority knew or should have known of the risk;
- The individual at risk is specifically identifiable;
- The individual was killed by the third party;
- The public authority failed to take reasonable steps that might have prevented the risk to life (note that the public authority need not be guilty of 'gross dereliction or wilful disregard of duty'): *Osman v UK* [1999] EHRR 245.

Article 2 also imposes a negative duty on the state not to deprive someone of life unless 'absolutely necessary' in the circumstances: *McCann v UK* [1996] 21 EHRR 97. Any deprivation of life by a private party or an agent of the state must be subject to the most careful and meaningful scrutiny before it can be justified in law.

A claim for breach of Article 2 may arise in the following situations:

- A racial killing that was preventable by a public authority (applying the *Osman* test);
- A death in custody (e.g. in a police station, prison or hospital);
- An extra-judicial killing by the agent of the state.

Article 3

Prohibition of Torture

Article 3 places a positive duty on the state to provide adequate protection to private individuals against the infliction of inhuman or degrading treatment by other private individuals.

In order for ill treatment to constitute a breach of Article 3, it must attain a 'minimum level of severity': *Ireland v UK* (1978) 2 EHRR 25. This will depend on its nature and extent, its physical and mental effects on the victim and personal matters such as the sex, age and state of health of the victim. Victims who are particularly vulnerable are entitled to protection by way of effective deterrence against serious breaches of their personal integrity.

Article 3 also imposes a negative duty on the state not to inflict any intense physical or mental suffering on a private individual. However, state-sanctioned punishment will only breach Article 3 if the level of humiliation or debasement involved exceeds that which is inherent in all punishment. As with Article 2, the state is under a duty to conduct a thorough and effective investigation into any alleged ill treatment that is purportedly in breach of Article 3.

A claim for breach of Article 3 may arise in the following situations:

- A racial attack where a public authority should have provided adequate protection but failed to do so;
- The use of force or the infliction of mental anguish by a public authority that was not made strictly necessary by the victim's own conduct or medical necessity;
- The failure of a public authority to investigate properly a legitimate complaint or prevent the foreseeable criminal acts of a third party.

Article 8

Right to Respect for Private and Family Life

The primary object of Article 8 is the protection of the privacy of the individual against arbitrary interference by public authorities. Article 8 also imposes a positive obligation on the state to provide for effective respect for private life. Significantly, the concept of private life covers the moral, psychological and physical integrity of the individual. It is certainly arguable that private life includes the right to live free from racial attack.

Article 8 is likely to provide fertile ground for creative legal challenges in the years ahead given the absence of a right to privacy under pre-HRA domestic law.

A claim for breach of Article 8 may arise in the following situations:

- Racial harassment by an employee of a public authority that hinders the victim's enjoyment of private life;
- The failure of a public authority to respect the pain, grief or distress caused by racial harassment and take effective action to deter its interference in the victim's private life.

Article 14

Prohibition of Discrimination

While Article 14 does not establish a separate and freestanding right to live free from discrimination, it does require the state to ensure that the individual's right to enjoy other Convention rights is equal. Consequently, as has been stated elsewhere in this book, it is an extremely important right in that it will widen the parameters of what forms of differentiation between individuals amount to discrimination in law.

In the context of this chapter, in order to succeed in a complaint of racial discrimination under Article 14 an applicant will have to prove beyond reasonable doubt that he or she was deprived of a Convention right as a result of the racial prejudice of a public authority: see *Velikova v Bulgaria* No. 41488/98, 18/5/00. This will be a difficult complaint to sustain, given the high standard of proof required and the fact that racial discrimination is usually more subtle than transparent.

A claim for breach of Article 14 (coupled with a claim for breach of another Convention right) may arise in the following situations:

- The failure of the police to prosecute racially motivated attacks or murders – breach of Article 2 and/or Article 3 and/or Article 8;
- Racially discriminatory stop-and-search practices by the police that disproportionately affect people from ethnic minority communities – breach of Article 8 and possibly Article 11 (freedom of assembly and association).

SECTION 3

WHO CAN CLAIM?

Any person who is a victim or any organisation that is a victim may pursue a claim under the HRA. This includes both present victims of racial harassment and their families and potentially those in danger of future attack as well.

SECTION 4

WHO IS LIABLE?

Victims of racial harassment will, for the most part, have grievances against public authorities for their inadequate response (or, in extreme cases, even their complicity with the perpetrators).

The distinction between pure and hybrid public authorities has been discussed elsewhere. In reality, this distinction will have little significance if the complaint is that a public authority failed to take effective action to combat racial harassment. Such a failure would clearly amount to an under-performance in the public functions of the authority. However, while private bodies fall outside the scope of the HRA, victims of racial harassment who have a legitimate grievance against a private body can complain that their human rights have been breached by the state for allowing the private body's conduct to go unpunished by the law.

SECTION 5

Case Study

Mr Khan contacts you. He and his family have been the victims of considerable racial harassment for a number of years. There have been incidents of physical violence, verbal abuse and criminal damage, all of which have been reported to the police. Despite the Khans identifying the perpetrators, the police have not arrested a single person. They have made various excuses – that neighbour disputes are best resolved between neighbours, that there is no independent evidence to support what the Khans allege, that the perpetrators are too young to prosecute, that the perpetrators have made counter-allegations against the Khans, and that to make a fuss would simply make matters worse.

The final straw was when Mr Khan's son Salim aged 15 was racially attacked by a white boy aged 17 and defended himself. Instead of arresting the white boy who was well known locally for being a racist and a bully, the police arrested Salim and charged him with assault occasioning actual bodily harm. Fortunately, Salim was acquitted at trial.

Mr Khan feels that his family's human rights have been violated. He wants to know what action can be taken against the perpetrators of racial harassment and the police. He also wants to know whether the HRA is of any use.

What do you advise?

Questions for consideration

1. Does Mr Khan want criminal proceedings to be taken against the perpetrators? If yes, does he want to continue putting pressure on the police to arrest and prosecute the perpetrators? Or does he want to pursue a private prosecution against the perpetrators?
2. Does Mr Khan want to pursue a civil action against the police for their general failure to protect his family from racial harassment? If yes, what causes of action under the amended RRA are in issue?
3. Does Salim Khan want to pursue a civil action against the police for arresting and prosecuting him? If yes, what causes of action under the amended RRA are in issue?
4. Is the HRA of any use against the perpetrators of racial harassment?
5. Is the HRA of any use against the police? Is it arguable that the police

have failed to act compatibly with the Convention rights of the Khans? If yes, what Convention rights are in issue?

Does the HRA make any real difference to the Khans? Does it materially affect the legal remedies that they can pursue against either the police or the perpetrators of racial harassment?

Housing law

Heather Williams

This chapter looks at the impact of the HRA on racial discrimination arising in relation to housing.

SECTION 1

POSITION PRE-HRA

The scope of the RRA

There can be little doubt that racism remains a prevalent problem, particularly for many on low incomes, in terms of obtaining decent housing and enjoying peaceful occupation of it. Before the HRA, the legal protection available to those on the receiving end of racist treatment in the housing field had been contained in the RRA. The HRA has added to but has not replaced this protection.

In the area of housing, the RRA operates by making unlawful racial discrimination in connection with certain specific acts. The main areas of conduct that the RRA covers are:

- s.21(1) RRA: refusing to sell or to let premises on a tenancy or to grant other rights of occupation, such as licences, in respect of them. Alternatively, making them available on comparatively adverse terms, for example at a higher rent or requiring a level of deposit that would not usually be sought. (There is an exception for owners who wholly occupy the premises and do not advertise or use an estate agent for the purposes of the disposal);
- s.21(2) RRA: treating occupiers unfairly in the way that they are given access to any benefits or facilities in relation to the premises, or refusing or deliberately failing to afford them access (for example, cutting off

heating, denying cleaning or maintenance services otherwise available);
- s.21(2) RRA: evicting occupiers or subjecting them to any other form of detriment. The latter is broadly interpreted and would include forms of harassment carried out by or on behalf of the landlord. It is also possible that it could cover a landlord's failure to take action against tenants causing harassment to another local resident, if the landlord had the means to control this, for example by use of powers in the tenancy agreements and/or the statutory powers referred to earlier in the last part of Chapter 2. However, this argument has yet to be tested in the courts; it would rely on drawing a parallel with cases decided in the employment context;
- s.24(1) RRA: refusing to consent to the proposed assignment of a tenancy or insisting upon it only taking place on comparatively adverse terms;
- s.20(1) RRA: refusing or deliberately omitting to provide, or providing on a comparatively adverse basis, short term accommodation usually made available for the public or a section of the public. This provision encompasses, for example, hotels, boarding houses, holiday camps and university halls of residence;
- s.21(1) RRA: adverse treatment in relation to any list of persons in need of premises of that description. This primarily applies to the operation of waiting lists for housing by local authorities and housing associations.

In each case, in order to establish unlawful conduct, it is necessary to show that the treatment complained of amounted to unlawful discrimination, i.e. direct discrimination, indirect discrimination or victimisation on racial grounds. These concepts have been explained in the Introduction. In this area of law, it means, for example, that a refusal to let premises to someone would only be unlawful if it could be proved that this was done on the grounds of their race or by applying a requirement with which a considerably smaller proportion of persons of that individual's racial group could comply (such as a requirement that persons have lived in the same area for a stated number of years). It is important to note that 'racial grounds' and 'racial group' are given a specific meaning in the RRA; it does not prohibit what might otherwise be unfair treatment that does not fall within these concepts.

The persons who would usually be sued under an RRA claim would be the owner of the premises in question or someone managing the premises on the owner's behalf (save where the claim related to the allocation of public sector housing). The legislation contains exceptions where the owner/manager or a near relative of his lives on the premises and shares accommodation with the person making the complaint or where someone is taken into another's home, as if a member of their family, because of their age, infirmity etc. The RRA does not provide a route for bringing a claim against fellow tenants/occupants for racist treatment.

Like many other areas discussed in this book, a claim under these provisions is complex to undertake and advisers should probably refer the case to, or work jointly with, lawyers specialising in this field. These provisions have not been widely used and have not had the impact that might have been hoped for in reducing discriminatory conduct in these areas.

The effect of the RR(A)A

The RR(A)A has broadened the circumstances in which discrimination claims can be brought against housing providers that are public authorities. The definition of public authorities is essentially the same as under the HRA (see the first two chapters). In housing terms, local authorities are public authorities for all purposes. Registered social landlords, such as housing associations, will sometimes be public authorities, depending upon their nature, structure and their particular functions that are under scrutiny (as discussed further in Section 4 of this Chapter).

All of a public authority's housing functions are now subject to claims of direct discrimination, indirect discrimination and victimisation. So, for example, difficulties will no longer arise as to whether certain local authority responsibilities, such as duties to the homeless or estate improvement schemes, can be brought within the wording of s.21 RRA, as they are plainly covered by the RR(A)A.

As explained earlier in Chapter 2, the RR(A)A also places duties on specified public authorities to have due regard to eliminating unlawful race discrimination and to promote equality of opportunity and good race relations. In the housing context the specified bodies upon whom these duties are currently imposed are local authorities, the Housing Corporation and Housing Action Trusts.

The way to complain

A complaint of racial discrimination under these provisions has to be made to a County Court. The case should be issued within six months of the date when the discrimination complained of took place: s.68(2) RRA. Where the act of discrimination is a continuing one, such as ongoing charging of an excessive rent, the six-month time limit does not start to run until the end of that period. Furthermore, the Court can extend these time limits if it feels that it is just and equitable to do so: s.68(6) RRA. The case is heard by a judge, but he or she may hear the case with assessors (persons having special knowledge and experience of race relations problems) if the parties so desire: s.67(4) RRA.

The person bringing the case has to show on a balance of probabilities that the discrimination complained of took place. This often makes it difficult to succeed; it is one thing to *suspect* that unfavourable treatment has occurred on racial grounds, quite another to *prove* it. However, the court may be prepared to draw inferences if comparatively unfavourable treatment has occurred and no alternative innocent explanation for it is put forward.

Legal aid is potentially available for funding a County Court discrimination claim, subject to the individual's means, the likely prospects of success and its likely value as against the likely costs of pursuing it. In practice the relatively low financial value of many potentially good claims precludes the possibility of legal aid funding, other than, possibly, for some initial advice and assistance. In particular if the claim is worth less than £5,000 it is vulnerable to being allocated to the 'small claims track' (unless complexity or the amount of evidence involved persuades the court otherwise). This will exclude the possibility of legal aid, although will mean that the person sued will be unlikely to be able to recover costs from the person bringing the claim, even if it ultimately fails. Where legal aid is not available, assistance can sometimes be sought from publicly funded organisations such as law centres or the CRE. This subject is discussed further in the chapter on funding.

Remedies

If the claim succeeds the court can award damages. The main heads of loss are likely to be injury to feelings and any financial loss resulting from the discrimination (for example, from time taken off work or expenses of finding alternative accommodation).

So far court awards for injury to feelings have not been particularly high and in most cases this part of the compensation would be unlikely to exceed several thousand pounds at the very best. One potential exception to this could be discriminatory conduct that had persisted over a lengthy period, for example long-term racial harassment by a landlord trying to get rid of a tenant. In such circumstances there may also be a substantial compensation claim for psychiatric injury. Another potential remedy is an injunction restraining the discriminator from continuing his or her unlawful behaviour or requiring them to act to put matters right, for example an order to re-admit a tenant evicted on racist grounds.

Restrictions on bringing a claim

The main factors inhibiting the extent to which the housing provisions of the RRA have been utilised have already been touched on in this Section. In summary they are:

1. The lack of public funding in many instances, save where the claim is substantial enough to attract legal aid;

2. The RRA does not cover all forms of what might generally thought to be racial discrimination in relation to housing, but only discrimination that:

- Falls within the concepts of direct discrimination, indirect discrimination or victimisation, which are all given a specific meaning in the RRA;
- Is on 'racial grounds' or on the basis of a person's 'racial group'. Again, these concepts are given a specific meaning in the RRA. The most notable effect of this is that groups identifiable as such by their religious beliefs alone will not be protected if discriminated against on these grounds (see the chapter on religious discrimination);
- Falls within the scope of the prohibited conduct, as summarised earlier in this Section;
- Is carried out by those who can be sued under the RRA. As discussed earlier this is predominantly owners or managers of premises in relation to their own acts or the conduct of those acting on their behalf.

The relative unfamiliarity of advisers with these provisions of the RRA and/or with County Court discrimination claims may, understandably, have contributed to the lack of claims brought in the past. Since it came into force, the HRA has presented new opportunities for legal challenge, for which advisers should be looking out.

SECTION 2

POSITION POST-HRA

The HRA expands the scope for challenging racial discrimination in relation to housing in the following ways. A new basis for bringing a claim arises where a public authority acts in a way that is incompatible with a Convention right, whether or not there is an existing right to sue under the RRA. The courts may be required to re-consider the way that they have applied the RRA in the past. In some instances, it will be possible to bring claims under both the RRA and under the HRA in the same proceedings.

The main articles of the Convention that are likely to be relevant in respect of racial discrimination and housing are:

Article 3

Prohibition of torture
As has been noted elsewhere in this book, this includes at least intentional harassment of a violent or highly oppressive character. It may be ripe for wider interpretation.

Article 8

Right to Respect for Private and Family Life

In the context of this chapter, 'home' has been widely interpreted by the ECommHR and ECtHR to include various forms of shelter such as caravans, provided the individual complainant owns or has other rights over the shelter. 'Respect for' has been taken to include the right of individuals to access, occupy and peacefully enjoy their accommodation, so any interference with these rights will come within Article 8. Early case law decided under the HRA confirms that Article 8 is also engaged when a court considers whether to deprive a person of accommodation by making a possession order. 'Respect for' may also include the rights of a minority group to respect for its particular lifestyle: G & E v Norway (1983) 35 DR 30. However, Article 8 has not generally been interpreted so as to give rise to a right to acquire any particular housing.

As has been noted elsewhere, conduct that appears to be a breach of Article 8 may be justified by the public authority if it can show that the interference is in accordance with the law, pursues one or more of the legitimate aims it lists and is necessary and proportionate.

Article 14

Prohibition of Discrimination

As has been noted elsewhere, it is important to note that the grounds upon which unlawful discrimination can arise under Article 14 are not limited to race and are much wider than under the RRA. The ECtHR has been slow to interpret this Article as including complaints of indirect discrimination, but this is an area that is potentially ripe for development.

Article 1 of Protocol 1

Protection of Property

The circumstances in which a public authority may justify its conduct under this provision are wider than under Article 8. Thus it is unlikely that a claim would succeed under this Article if it had failed under Article 8.

Examples of the HRA in Operation

Advisers should consider whether circumstances give rise to a claim under the HRA, particularly where a claim under the RRA would not or may not be viable or has yet to be tested. This could include:

- Racial harassment carried out by tenants of a public authority against someone living in the locality (whether or not they are a tenant of the public authority themselves). If the level of harassment is substantial, Article 3 and/or Article 8 places a positive duty on the authority to secure the individual's rights by taking reasonable steps to provide adequate protection against it. If the victim can show that the authority has failed in this duty a claim would arise. As indicated earlier in this Chapter, it is unclear whether a claim under RRA would succeed in these circumstances;

- Local authority determinations of homelessness applications pursuant to rules, requirements or practices that have an adverse impact on persons from particular racial or religious groups. For example, where extended families are not treated as a single unit for the purposes of determining whether they are homeless or for what amounts to an offer of suitable accommodation; or the way that accommodation in another part of the world is evaluated as potentially available for the applicant's occupation. If a discriminatory impact on persons of certain races can be shown, consider a claim under Article 14 in conjunction with Article 8;

- Discrimination against tenants (or would-be tenants) by public authorities on religious grounds or quasi-race grounds falling outside the definition of 'racial grounds' and 'racial groups' in the RRA, but potentially within Article 14 read with Article 8 (at least as regards those who have been deprived of accommodation). It might be expected that instances of indirect, rather than direct, discrimination would be more common so far as public authorities are concerned. In this regard consider, for example, restrictions in tenancy agreements as to user of accommodation that inhibit certain forms of lifestyle or worship;

- The housing of asylum-seekers under the IAA. Under these provisions the National Asylum Support Service disperses asylum-seekers to parts of the country where they may have no community ties, are vulnerable to overt racism from local inhabitants and are far away from meaningful practical and legal assistance. Consider if a discriminatory impact can be shown as regards persons of certain races and whether a claim under Article 14 in conjunction with Article 8, or possibly Article 3, arises;

- In extreme circumstances, for example where a client has suffered very bad harassment and is in ill health as a result, consider using Articles 3 and/or 8 to argue for a right to obtain alternative accommodation provided by the relevant local authority. The RRA confers no such positive rights and such an argument could be useful if the individual did not meet the criteria for accommodation under housing or community care legislation;

- Circumstances where public authority tenants are unable to exercise their rights effectively as a result of problems linked to their race, for example a difficulty in complaining about disrepair to their accommodation to the local neighbourhood office because of a language barrier. A claim of indirect discrimination could arise under Article 14 in conjunction with Article 8. This line of argument could also augment a claim based on a broad interpretation of s.21(2)(a) RRA where private tenants are concerned;

- Aspects of the Housing Benefit (General) Regulations 1987 are vulnerable to challenge as incompatible with the Convention. Regulation 7(1) treats an individual as not liable to make a payment for his or her dwelling where it is made to a fellow resident who is a close relative. Arguably this has a racial discriminatory impact upon those whose culture tends towards living as part of an extended family. Advisers should consider carefully whether any relevant subordinate legislation is vulnerable to being struck down as a result of its racially discriminatory effect.

A further point to be aware of is that, more generally, decision-making in relation to public sector housing is likely to be highly vulnerable to claims under Article 6 of the Convention, based on the lack of any independent and impartial determination of applications on their merits. While such challenges may arise in relation to local authority determinations that have no relation to racial discrimination issues, it could be a useful additional argument to consider in a case that does raise such matters.

As explained earlier, the HRA can also have a significant effect in a claim brought by one individual against another private individual, for example where a tenant sues his private sector landlord for evicting him on racist grounds. The Claimant will be able to argue that the Court should reconsider its past interpretation of the RRA in the light of the Convention. This could lead, for example, to a wider interpretation of 'racial grounds' or 'racial group' so as to include those religious or quasi-racial groups thus far held to fall outside its terms.

The HRA could also ground a defence to a local authority possession claim if the basis upon which possession was sought was open to challenge as directly or indirectly discriminatory, for example allegations of nuisance based upon conduct reflecting a particular culture or lifestyle or rent arrears arising through the operation of discriminatory housing benefit provisions (see above).

SECTION 3

WHO CAN CLAIM?

As has been explained elsewhere in this book, a freestanding claim under the HRA can be brought by anyone who is (or would be) a victim of actions made unlawful by the Act. In the housing context, this will generally be the individual who has been discriminated against. However, in some circumstances a representative body such as a tenant's organisation could be a 'victim'.

SECTION 4

WHO IS LIABLE?

Certain bodies are clearly public authorities and thus can be sued under the HRA. In the housing context, local authorities are the most obvious example. Claims against them can be brought in relation to the discharge of any of their functions.

Equally, there are landlords and other bodies or individuals concerned with housing that are not public authorities within the meaning of the HRA. This includes individuals or many companies who rent out property for profit.

As discussed in Section 1, it is possible that certain housing associations fall within the third category of 'hybrid' public authorities, depending upon the extent to which the conduct under challenge concerns the discharge of their public (as opposed to private) functions. The more that a particular association carries out functions that were previously undertaken by local authorities, the greater the likelihood that it will be susceptible to challenge under the HRA. Advisers must always consider carefully the particular treatment that is being criticised. If, for example, it relates solely to the terms of an individual's tenancy agreement, this may well be regarded as a purely private, contractual function. However, if it relates to rules for the allocation of housing or consultation over the development of housing, it is possible that a sufficiently public character to the functions would be present. For example, the Court of Appeal recently decided that the Poplar Housing Association was a public authority for the purposes of the HRA when providing accommodation in fulfilment of the local authority's duties to the homeless, that had previously been owned by the local authority: *Donoghue v Poplar HARCAL* [2001] EWCA Civ 595.

The fact that the housing provider is not a public authority will not preclude either:

- Claims against a public authority that has breached its positive obligations owed to the individual to protect his or her Convention rights from
interference by other private individuals or bodies; or
- The provisions of the Convention affecting the manner in which the
court interprets the legal position between private individuals in dispute.

Practical features

Practical matters of particular relevance to housing-related race problems
are as follows:

- Consider in each case whether a human rights angle arises by way of
one or more of the routes set out above. As well as creating a new claim
or bolstering an existing one, use of the HRA is likely to enhance opportunities for publicity and increase the pressure upon the other party.
Many organisations vulnerable to a great breadth of claims under the
HRA, such as local authorities, are likely to be quite wary of adverse
decisions being made against them under the HRA, particularly in the
early period of its operation when they may be relatively unfamiliar with
its scope;
- Consider the possibility of legal aid funding or assistance from publicly
funded organisations in each case. The 'useful addresses' section at the
end may prove helpful in finding finance;
- Many of the issues that are likely to arise in the housing area are relatively un-tested, in the sense that there has not been much previous
case law before the ECtHR raising these sorts of issues. The scope for
constructive development is therefore substantial but test cases should
be chosen carefully. As this is a relatively complex area advisers will
need to consider obtaining specialist legal assistance.

SECTION 5

Case Study

The problem

The Ahmed family live in their own accommodation on the Monckton Estate
in central Dourbridge. The bulk of the estate comprises properties owned by
the Homely Housing Association, which are rented out to tenants on low
incomes. Over the last year and a half the Ahmed family have experienced
repeated racist harassment, including offensive graffiti on their front door
and external walls and obscenities and threats shouted through the front
door, referring to their effect upon the neighbourhood. Their children have

been followed and abused in the area of the premises. Recently an anonymous note containing a death threat was pushed through the letterbox. The Ahmed family have spoken to the Housing Association, which says that, whilst they of course deplore such behaviour, as far as they are concerned there is no evidence that the perpetrators are their tenants, and in any event they would not be liable for these actions even if this could be shown.

Questions for consideration

If you are consulted by the Ahmed family as to what if any action they can take against the Housing Association (as opposed to the police, for which see elsewhere in this book), consider:

1. Would a remedy have been likely under the pre-HRA law? Possibly, but this is untested.
2. Is the Homely Housing Association a 'public authority' under the HRA for present purposes? Possibly.
3. If it is, is there a potential claim against it under the HRA? Yes: by virtue of Articles 3 and/or 8, the Association may be under a positive duty to take reasonable steps to afford protection to the Ahmed family, by using their statutory powers and the provisions of their tenancy agreements to control their tenants. Simply waiting for the Ahmed family to produce any concrete evidence of a link to their tenants, when they own and let out so much of the surrounding estate, is unlikely to be sufficient.
4. What action should be taken initially? The Association should be contacted and its obligations under the HRA pointed out. They should take reasonable steps to identify the perpetrators and, if a link is made to their tenants, they should act to prevent further problems, for example by enforcing the provisions of their tenancy agreements with the harassers. Publicity could also assist.
5. What is the limitation position? The harassment has continued for over a year – though the housing authority may have been on notice of it and thus in breach of their obligations for a shorter period. In order to maximise the period for which damages may be claimed, proceedings should be issued fairly swiftly.
6. Is legal aid or other publicly funded assistance available? Possibly, see the section of funding elsewhere in the book.
7. What evidence should be gathered? Take witness statements from those involved promptly. Advise them to keep a diary of future incidents. Consider obtaining medical evidence of the effects upon the family to strengthen the Article 3 argument. Care will need to be taken to obtain relevant documentation from the Association in due course.

Actions against the police

Sadiq Khan

This chapter examines the role that the HRA will play in combating racial discrimination in cases involving police misconduct.

SECTION 1

POSITION PRE-HRA

Before the HRA came into force, the legal framework for taking actions against the police was as follows.

Complaint

This involves a complaint being made to the police who investigate their colleagues. The Police Complaints Authority has been set up since the mid-1980s to supervise the investigation of serious cases and to supervise the bringing or consideration of disciplinary or criminal charges in all cases other than those that are informally resolved. In addition, the PCA has powers to supervise the investigation of non-complaint matters voluntarily referred to it by the police such as a shooting incident, deaths in police custody and cases of serious corruption. It is important to note that it is always the police who investigate the police and that supervision by the PCA only occurs in a small minority of cases.

If the complaint is upheld, it is possible for a police officer to be disciplined and/or criminally prosecuted. It is important to bear in mind that it is only a small minority of complaints that are ever upheld and that a client's expectations should not be raised with regard to making a complaint.

Civil litigation

The other option open to a complainant in addition to or instead of making a complaint is to sue the police for a civil wrong (a tort). This is an expensive option and can only really be done if the complainant is entitled to receive funding from the Legal Services Commission. If the complaint is of racial discrimination then the CRE can advise and may offer legal representation. Some trade unions may also consider paying the legal costs of bringing a case against the police. It is not currently possible to obtain insurance cover for such actions.

Aside from racial discrimination claims, the torts that are relevant in cases against the police are:

* Assault and battery;
* False imprisonment;
* Malicious prosecution;
* Malicious process;
* Negligence;
* Trespass to land;
* Seizure of goods; and
* Misfeasance in public office.

If the complainant alleges either false imprisonment and/or malicious prosecution, then this may entitle him/her to a trial before a Judge and Jury. Otherwise, the trial is before a Judge only in a County Court or High Court.

If a complainant is successful in a civil action against the police, then he or she is entitled to damages and legal costs. There have been cases where, as a result of a successful civil action, the police have agreed to investigate the conduct of officers as a result of the evidence that came out at a trial. However, this is extremely rare.

Note that the ECommHR held in the case of Govell v UK [1999] EHRLR 121 that a police complaint in a bugging case did not constitute an effective remedy for the purposes of Article 13. This was because the Police Complaints Authority was not deemed to be a sufficiently independent body!

The way to complain

Any member of the public can make a complaint; it need not be the victim. So, for example, a person witnessing an officer assaulting someone in the street can make a complaint.

The complaint needs to be made to the police. If a complaint is made orally, a police officer will interview the complainant and draft a statement for him or her to sign. Complainants should be advised to go to a solicitor who can draft a statement on a complainant's behalf and forward this on to the police and to the Police Complaints Authority. The advantage of this is that this avoids any misunderstanding or confusion. Indeed, there is a risk that complainants who attempt to make oral complaints may not have their complaints recorded.

Further, complainants sometimes feel that a statement written for them by police officers are not in their own words or what they meant. It is important to bear in mind that the statement can be used at a subsequent disciplinary hearing and will be disclosed should there be a civil action against the police. Any differences between the complainant's statement and a subsequent statement given for the civil action may be used to discredit the complainant.

A complaint should be made within a year of the incident being complained about. If a complaint is made more than a year after the incident, the police may refuse to investigate the complaint. As soon as the complaint is made, the police officers against whom the complaint is made are served a Notice informing them that a complaint has been made. The investigating officer then interviews any witnesses and obtains any medical reports and evidence, and finally will interview the officers concerned.

Should there be a civil action against the police, all the documents generated by a complaint (except for the investigating officer's report) will be disclosable in the civil action.

As a result of a recent change in the Police Disciplinary Codes, the burden of proof now required to uphold a complaint is on the balance of probabilities. In other words: was it more likely than not that the alleged incident took place?

Should a disciplinary hearing be held, the complainant will be allowed to be present with a friend or relative. The hearings are held in private.

The way to bring a civil action against the police

Although it is not obligatory to use a solicitor to sue the police, it is recommended. It is important to remember that, in civil litigation, the basic rule is that the 'loser pays the winner's costs'. This means that, if the complainant (claimant) sues the police privately and is unsuccessful, he or she will have to pay the police's legal costs as well as his or her own legal costs. Claimants who receive legal aid are usually protected from an adverse order of costs against them should they be unsuccessful in the claim.

Most torts against the police have a limitation period of six years from the date of the incident. However, it is recommended to bring a civil action as soon as the case papers are ready, as memories often diminish of witnesses and claimants can be criticised for delay in bringing an action.

A claimant needs to send a letter of claim to the police setting out the basis of his or her claim including details of any injuries suffered. The police then have three months to respond to this claim and provide the claimant with disclosure of relevant documents. If the claimant is unhappy with the response from the Defendant, he or she can issue proceedings in either the County Court or High Court.

The RR(A)A makes a Police Force vicariously liable for the racially discriminatory acts of police officers committed in the course of their employment. It is important to note that the time limits for bringing claims under the RRA are different to time limits for civil claims. Advisers will need to consider how best to proceed in a claim where there has been both racial discrimination (either direct or indirect) by the police and another tort. Also, the principles of damages will be different.

Medical reports

If there is a claim for physical or psychiatric injury then a claimant will need to obtain a medical report. If the complainant has suffered injuries, it is advisable to see a doctor as soon as possible, so that a record of the injuries is taken. Photographs of any injuries should also be taken.

Compensation

The court can award compensation in a successful claim against the police. For clients whose claim includes a claim for false imprisonment and/or malicious prosecution, the Jury will award damages based upon guidance given by the Judge. This guidance derives from a Court of Appeal case, *Hsu & Thompson v Commissioner of Police for the Metropolis* (Times, 20/02/1997), which sets out the level of damages to be awarded. Damages are broken down into three areas; basic damages; aggravated damages; and exemplary damages.

Basic damages

In a straightforward case for wrongful arrest and false imprisonment, the starting point for basic damages is likely to be at £500 for the first hour for detention. Someone kept in custody for 24 hours in a straightforward case is entitled to an award of about £3,000.

If there were any medical injuries, the Courts will use the guidelines laid down by the Judicial Studies Board, which has a tariff depending on the injury sustained.

In a case of malicious prosecution, the basic award starts at about £2,000. For malicious prosecutions that continued for as long as two years before being taken to the Crown Court, an award of about £10,000 is appropriate.

Aggravated damages

These are awarded when there are aggravating features about the case, which would result in the claimant not receiving sufficient compensation for the injuries suffered if the award were restricted to a basic award. Aggravating features have been said to include 'humiliating circumstances at the time of the arrest or any conduct of those responsible for the arrest or the prosecution, which showed that they behaved in a high-handed, insulting, malicious or oppressive manner ...'.

Aggravated damages are unlikely to be less than £1,000 and would not be more than twice the basic damages except where the basic damages are modest.

Exemplary damages
This is awarded to punish the police where there has been conduct that is oppressive or arbitrary.

Exemplary damages are between £5,000 and £25,000. If a very senior police officer is involved, up to £50,000 can be awarded.

SECTION 2

POSITION POST-HRA

In cases against the police, all pre-HRA rights remain in place but the new rights of relevance available are as follows. Before setting them out, it should be remembered that existing Strasbourg case law covers many of these issues. As in many other areas discussed in this book, the primary role of these rights will be to augment existing rights by allowing individuals to raise fresh arguments wherever possible, often combining them with an existing claim under a tort.

Article 2

Right to Life
Article 2 imposes two duties on the State (and its officials). The first, not to deprive anyone of his/her life save in the limited circumstances prescribed by Article 2(2). Second, to take reasonable measures to protect life.

In this context, consider:

- Those who have been killed in situations where the State (or its officials) were aware of the risk and failed to take effective action to deter the commission of offences against the victim;
- Those who have been killed by the police in shooting incidents;
- Those who die in State custody e.g. police, prisons, mental health institutions.

Article 3

Prohibition of Torture

Article 3 provides that no one shall be subjected to torture or to inhumane or degrading treatment or punishment.

The ECtHR and ECommHR has found many forms of conduct to be *capable* of breaching Article 3, including: serious assaults, particularly assaults in custody; the application of psychological interrogation techniques; prison conditions; rape; corporal punishment; extradition or expulsion where torture or ill-treatment might be a consequence.

In this context, consider:

- Those alleging assault and battery against officials of the State (police officers, prison officials, nurses);
- Deaths in police custody;
- Those who are detained either in prison, mental institutions or police stations;
- 'Restraint methods' and techniques used by police officers, prison officials, nurses;
- The excessive use of handcuffs/batons/CS spray.

Article 5

The Right to Liberty and Security of the Person

Article 5 has two limbs: it guarantees liberty and security of persons; and it provides a set of procedural rights for detainees.

In domestic law any confinement of an individual, however short, amounts to a deprivation of liberty and is unlawful: see the tort of false imprisonment. Under the Convention, the position is different. An arrest will of course trigger Article 5 protection. However, where the exercise of police powers falls short of arrest, but nonetheless prevents an individual from doing what he or she would like, the position is less clear-cut. Stop and search is an example. Accordingly, the meaning of 'deprivation of liberty' can be crucial in cases involving the exercise of stop and search and similar powers.

The period of detention is relevant, but not definitive. Where police officers (or any other public officials) take action that deprives individuals of their liberty, their *objective* will usually be the crucial factor. If the objective is to detain, Article 5 applies. If there is some other objective, those actions will have to be carefully examined to see whether, in effect, they amount to a deprivation of liberty within the meaning of Article 5.

In this context, consider:

- PACE requirements;
- Patterns suggesting that young black men are being stopped and searched by police officers without being arrested or charged;
- Cases where an arrest takes place in the absence of reasonable suspicion;
- Cases where the police rely upon confidential information and anonymous sources to justify arrest;
- Cases when an arrested person does not speak or understand English properly, and so does not understand the reasons for his or her arrest.

Article 6

Right to a Fair Trial

Article 6(1) applies to both criminal and civil proceedings whereas Articles 6(2) and 6(3) apply to criminal proceedings only.

Article 6(1) lists the minimum requirements of a fair trial. Civil actions against the police amount to the determination of civil rights and obligations, and so the fair trial obligations of Article 6(1) apply. These include the right to an independent and impartial tribunal, the right to disclosure, the right to an adversarial hearing, the right to a reasoned decision and the right to trial within a reasonable period.

In this context, consider:

- If the police are claiming immunity from negligence proceedings;
- The removal of civil legal aid from civil actions against the police;
- The failure to grant legal aid or the choice of the client's own solicitor;
- Cases where the police have information from an informant but refuse to disclose the statement and/or call this person to give evidence at a trial.

Article 8

The Right to Respect or Private and Family Life

Article 8 affects the private life, family life, the home and correspondence.

The taking and retention of personal data, such as fingerprints, photographs and DNA samples raise a number of major issues under Article 8. Searches, taking personal details and/or photographs of suspects interferes with their privacy and must be justified under Article 8(2). Police searches must be justified under Article 8(2). The use of undercover agents in police investigations raises two issues under the Convention: fair trial (Article 6) and privacy (Article 8).

In this context, consider:

- Police surveillance, including the use of CCTV cameras and bugging devices, although this is now separately regulated by RIPA; and
- Police officers taking photographs of individuals on the street without arresting or detaining the individuals.

Article 14

Prohibition of Discrimination
As has been stated elsewhere, Article 14 confers no freestanding right to be free of discrimination on the various stated grounds, but relates only to the enjoyment of other Convention rights without discrimination. It is only necessary for the individuals to have raised an issue coming within the ambit of other Convention rights. Accordingly, advisers should consider whether a claim under Article 14 could be made in circumstances where issues under any of the other Articles of the Convention have been raised.

SECTION 3

WHO CAN CLAIM?

Claims under the HRA can be brought by anyone who is (or would be) a victim of an act made unlawful by the HRA. The victim can be any legal entity. In the context of this chapter, this will mostly mean those who have suffered from an abuse of power by the police, the prison service or other bodies exercising similar power.

SECTION 4

WHO IS LIABLE?

This is more straightforward than in many of the other areas discussed in this book, as police forces are unequivocally organs of the State and so can be sued under the HRA as public authorities in connection with all their functions.

Practical issues
Many practical matters are dealt with more fully elsewhere in this book, but those of particular relevance in relation to actions against the police are:

1. Always look for the human rights angle in connection with police misconduct.

2. Think laterally in looking for human rights issues: many are not obviously a breach of human rights, but have a human rights angle. Do not forget the limitation period for bringing proceedings under the HRA.
3. If there is a human rights angle, then the claimant is more likely to receive funding from the Legal Services Commission.

SECTION 5

Case Study
The Smith family have a dispute with their neighbours. The neighbours hurl racial abuse at the Smith family. The Smith family telephoned the Police as they are concerned for their personal safety. The Police arrive at the scene and after speaking to the Smith family and the neighbours (who are white) decide to arrest Wayne Smith who is 17 years old, for an offence of the Public Order Act. He is taken to the local Police station. Mr Smith (Wayne's father) telephones the Police station to make a complaint about the fact that his son has been arrested when he was the Complainant. He later arrives at the Police station front desk to find out how his son is and to give further details of his complaint. However, at the front desk there are heated words and Mr Smith is arrested for a Public Order Offence. During his detention at the Police station Wayne is put in the same cell as two individuals who have Swastikas tattooed on their arms. Wayne is seriously assaulted in this Police cell and is hospitalised and is placed on a life support machine. After two weeks Wayne died. Mr Smith is released from Police custody the following day and charged with an offence under the Public Order Act and at his criminal trial he is acquitted.

Questions for consideration
The Smith family consults you as to what, if any, action they can take against the Police (as opposed to others mentioned above). Consider;

1. Would a remedy have been unlikely under the pre-HRA law? Yes – 1. Civil action against the Police, 2. Police complaint, 3. Claim under RRA.
2. Is the Police a 'Public Authority' under the HRA for present purposes? Yes.
3. If it is, is there a potential claim against it under the HRA? Yes – see Articles 2, 3, 6, 14.
4. What action should be taken? The estate of the deceased has a separate claim from Mr Smith senior. The number of overlapping potential claims available 1. Police complaint? 2. Civil action against the Police

(stand alone or with HRA claim added). 3. Human Rights Act claim (stand alone or with civil action). 4. RRA claim.

5. What is the limitation position? Depends on course of action: Police complaint – within 12 months, RRA – within 6 months, HRA claim – stand alone – within 1 year, substantive tort – within 6 years.
6. Is legal aid or other publicly funded assistance available? Yes.
7. What evidence should be gathered? Contemporaneous document will be invaluable at any trial. e.g. medical notes, photographs, notes made at the time (will be able to obtain disclosure of all the Police documents).
8. What remedy does Mr Smith senior have? He has his own potential claim against the Police for the way he has been treated (RRA).

Employment law

Barry Clarke

This chapter examines the role played by the HRA in combating racial discrimination in the employment field.

SECTION 1
POSITION PRE-HRA

The contract of employment

The relationship between an employer and an employee is regulated by a private contract of employment. The contract should specify such matters as job title, the rate of pay, holiday entitlement, provisions for sick pay, provisions for the giving of notice, and so on. Ideally, the contract should be in writing, but this is not always the case.

A feature of many contracts – and especially the contract of employment – is that its parties have unequal bargaining power. Inevitably, in most cases, it is the employer who will be in the position of strength. Very few employees can dictate the level of pay they receive, the amount of their holiday entitlement or, even whether they will be treated fairly.

The role of employment law

This is where employment law comes in. A highly regulated area of law with a large number of relevant statutes and statutory instruments, it attempts to ensure that employees are treated lawfully by giving them a floor of basic rights above and beyond those in the contract of employment.

The extent to which employment law succeeds in providing this floor of rights, and the role that employment law should play in regulating what is essentially a private relationship, are both matters for debate. Any person with a passing interest in this area will know where the battle lines are drawn between employer organisations and trade unions.

The law also regulates the extent to which workers from other countries outside the EU can take up employment in the UK, through the work permit system. The Government recently announced proposals to refine the work permit scheme in order to facilitate the movement of foreign nationals into work areas where there are currently skills shortages. The work permit scheme is beyond the scope of this chapter, save to note that many have observed that it operates to the advantage of migrant workers from 'Westernised' countries.

The RRA

Anti-discrimination law plays a very important part in helping to provide this floor of basic rights. When interacting with employment law, it provides a legal basis for attempting to ensure that employees are treated equally. It does this by making it unlawful to discriminate against employees on certain prohibited grounds, such as sex, race and disability. The most important anti-racial discrimination measures in the employment field are set out in Part II of the RRA, which is designed to ensure that the relationship between an employer and an employee is not tainted by discrimination on racial grounds. The rights are bestowed on both job applicants and current employees and, in the latter case, can include contract workers.

As for job applicants, employers cannot discriminate against them on racial grounds:

- In the arrangements made for determining who should be offered employment;
- In the terms on which employment is offered; or
- By refusing employment.

The Information Commissioner has suggested that using personal data in the process of appointing employees in a discriminatory fashion could also involve a breach of the DPA. At the time of publication of this book, the Information Commissioner had issued the 'Employment Practices Data Protection Code'. It is well worth a read for those who wish to understand how protection of data is or should be handled in the employment relationship.

As for current employees, employers cannot discriminate against them on racial grounds:

- In the terms under which they are employed;
- In the way they are provided with access to opportunities for promotion, transfer or training, and any other benefits; or
- By dismissing them or subjecting them to any other detriment (such as racial harassment).

Further detail on how the RRA operates has been given in the introduction and the separate chapter on the state of existing anti-discrimination legislation. It is a complex area of law and advisers should be encouraged to refer the case to, or work jointly with, a lawyer specialising in this field. It is vital to emphasis that the RRA will continue to be the main source of redress for individuals who consider that their employers have racially discriminated against them.

The key main types of legal claims will continue to be those provided for in the RRA: direct discrimination, indirect discrimination and victimisation, which have all been explained elsewhere in this book.

Indirect discrimination claims tend to be more common in gender equality rather than racial equality cases (for example, cases involving discrimination against part-time workers or those with childcare responsibilities). In the field of racial equality, direct discrimination and victimisation claims are more common, often relating to allegations of unequal treatment in terms of appointment and promotion.

In turn, many direct discrimination cases involve allegations of racial harassment against co-workers. Regrettably, the law offers a rather tortuous route to establishing liability for an employer and a co-worker in such circumstances. The employer is deemed to have carried out the racial harassment itself, and so has what the courts have called a 'constructive liability' for such harassment. The employee is not directly liable for the harassment, but can be joined as a respondent to an Employment Tribunal complaint (see below) on the basis that he or she 'aided' the employer's constructive liability. Trying to work out which liability arises first is a bit like determining the provenance of the proverbial chicken and egg and, in practice, it is rarely subject to detailed analysis by Tribunals.

The RRA provides a defence to an employer if it can show that it took such steps as were reasonably practicable to prevent its workers from behaving in a harassing manner. It is unlikely to be enough for an employer to point to the existence of an 'Equal Opportunities Policy' as satisfying this defence. If it cannot make out that defence, it will be liable for such workplace harassment. The Court of Appeal has recently confirmed that, even if the employer makes out this defence, the co-worker may remain personally liable under the 'aiding' provisions discussed above; see *Yeboah v Crofton* [2002] IRLR 634.

It is worth noting here that the RR(A)A has had a particular impact upon cases of racial harassment brought by one police officer against another. The issue of the constructive liability of the Chief Constable of a police force, for the racial harassment of one police officer of another before the RR(A)A came into force, has recently been tested in the appeal courts (see *Liversidge v Chief Constable of Bedfordshire Police* [2002], IRLR 651). Legal advice should be sought in such cases.

The RR(A)A has also had a more general impact upon public sector employment. With effect from 3 December 2001, for example, public sector employers have been under a legal obligation to monitor staff ethnicity. Employers were given until 31 May 2002 to devise and complete a race equality scheme explaining how they intended to monitor race issues within the workplace. Employers with more than 150 staff must also ensure that staff recruitment and promotion is not in any way related to discriminatory racial preferences. Employers are also required to check and analyse performance appraisals, disciplinary actions, dismissals and resignations. Furthermore, in October 2002, the DTI issued for consultation the draft Race Relations 1976 (Amendment) Regulations 2003, the purpose of which will be to implement the new EC Race Directive by the required date of 19 July 2003. The most important effect of the Regulations will be to introduce a revised definition of indirect discrimination, a new definition of harassment, and a shifting in the burden of proof.

The RRA also allows individuals to take claims of racial discrimination against the trade unions of which they are members, although this chapter will not focus on this aspect. It is worth pointing out that poor service from a union is not necessarily the same as discriminatory treatment, but may still give rise to an ordinary claim for negligence.

The role of the HRA will be to augment these existing rights by allowing individuals to raise fresh arguments wherever possible, perhaps combining them with an existing claim under the RRA.

The way to complain

Individuals who feel that their employers have unlawfully discriminated against them on racial grounds have the right to present a complaint to an Employment Tribunal. In cases of workplace racial harassment, it is often advisable to join in individual harassers as parties to the complaint, despite the tortuous legal basis for doing so described above. Appeals are presented to the Employment Appeal Tribunal.

It is important to remember that, with only limited exceptions, there is a three-month time limit for presenting Employment Tribunal complaints. The time limit usually runs from the date of the last act of alleged discrimination (such as the last act of harassment or the date of a racially-motivated dismissal), and may be brought with an additional complaint such as unfair dismissal. The Tribunal has the power to extend this time limit in certain cases, but it is very unwise to rely on it doing so. The time limit will not necessarily be extended just because an employee is making use of an internal grievance procedure.

An individual may also wish to ask his or her employer probing questions about its approach to race equality. The RRA provides a very helpful basis for doing so: the statutory questionnaire. The individual must explain the basis on which he or she thinks they have suffered discrimination, and may seek an explanation from the employer. Supplemental questions may then be asked about all manner of things, such as ethnic monitoring, recruitment and promotion procedures, equal opportunities training, and so on. A questionnaire may be served on an employer at any time prior to making a

Tribunal complaint, and within 21 days of lodging the complaint at Tribunal.

At the Tribunal hearing, it is for the individual complaining to establish, on the balance of probabilities, that the alleged discrimination has taken place. This can often make it difficult to win those types of case in which it is simply the word of the employee against the word of his or her employer. In fact, it is common in factually complex racial discrimination cases for the applicant to be his or her only main witness. It is also common for applicants to possess no clear evidence of obvious racial discrimination when presenting complaints, which means that Tribunals are usually invited to draw *inferences* of racial discrimination from the primary facts presented to them. Much will depends on the inferences which the Tribunal thinks it right to draw from the evidence put before it, and from the way the employer responded to any statutory questionnaire served on it. This means that the manner in which the case is presented can be crucial to the prospects of success.

Remedies

If an applicant is successful in a claim, the Tribunal can make a declaration that he or she has been racially discriminated against. A declaration can sometimes mean more to an applicant than money, and its importance should not be overlooked. The Tribunal may also recommend steps that an employer should take to reduce the adverse effect of the discrimination (such as an apology or revised recruitment practices); if that recommendation is not carried out, further compensation may be awarded.

The Tribunal can also award financial compensation for a successful complaint of racial discrimination. An award of compensation is usually made up of the financial loss the individual has suffered as a consequence of the discrimination (such as, in the case of a racially-motivated dismissal, lost earnings) and an award for what is called 'hurt feelings' or 'injured feelings'. In exceptional cases, it can include damages for personal or psychiatric injury caused by the act of racial discrimination.

Lost earnings, including lost pension rights, can produce a sizeable award, sometimes (although rarely) in six figures. Unlike in unfair dismissal cases brought under the ERA, there is no ceiling on the amount of compensation that is payable. However, it is important to bear in mind that high awards for lost earnings will not be made unless an applicant is out of work for a very long period, either through ill health, advanced age or a justifiable inability to find alternative work.

However, where an applicant is claiming racial discrimination against his or her *current* employer, there will often be no lost earnings at all (except perhaps in connection with time off sick). In those cases, it is important to bear in mind that the award will be for injured feelings only. Although occasionally very high (six figure sums have been made), these are usually quite modest. It is extremely difficult to give precise indications, but a one-off racist remark defended as 'office banter' may result in an injured feelings award of only a few hundred pounds, while an ongoing process of harassment may result in an award of several thousand pounds.

So, when carrying out the important task of managing a client's expectations, it should be borne in mind that racial discrimination cases in the employment field can often result in low compensation. The total annual payout for all types of discrimination in 2000 was £3.53 million, but the average award for racial discrimination remains low at between £10,000 and £15,000. Awards for injured feelings are subsumed within this figure, but the median award for injured feelings in racial discrimination cases in 2000 was only £3,000 (compared with £2,000 for sex discrimination cases and £2,500 for disability discrimination cases). In 2000, there was only one award for injury to feelings (including aggravated damages) in excess of £30,000.

Also, although one would hope to receive identical treatment from each and every Tribunal, the reality is that the outcome of a case and the sum awarded will sometimes vary according to the Tribunal members, and not simply the quality of the client's evidence.

In theory, awards can also be made against co-workers who have been identified in the Tribunal complaint as respondents. When this happens, an employer may indemnify the co-worker, although such awards tend in any event to be modest.

Limitations

There are four important limitations to the RRA to bear in mind in the context of this chapter.

First, there is very little public funding for RRA cases. Assistance can sometimes be sought from advice groups or publicly funded organisations such as law centres or the Commission for Racial Equality (see the chapter on funding later in this book).

Secondly, as mentioned in the introduction, the RRA deals only with discrimination on racial grounds under the heads of direct discrimination, indirect discrimination and victimisation. There is no reference to other forms of racism that individuals may encounter, such as 'institutional racism' as defined within the Macpherson report. This means that, when dealing with a client who feels that he or she is a victim of institutional racism, advisers should consider into which category of discrimination recognised by the RRA the complaint falls.

Thirdly, a point that has been made elsewhere in this book, the definition of protected racial groups in the RRA fails to refer adequately to the role that a person's religious beliefs can play in determining his or her racial identity. As a result, Muslim and Rastafarian individuals have not been recognised as being part of racial groups because, it is said, their religious beliefs do not provide a basis for a *racial* identity. By contract, Sikh and Jewish individuals are recognised by British law as having a distinct racial identity.

Finally, whereas the impetus for much of the reforming legislation in the sex discrimination field has come from Europe, this is not the case with racial discrimination legislation. The treaties that form the basis of the European Union clearly set out that there should be equal treatment for men and women at work. However, there are no similar EU provisions setting out the basis for equal treatment at work for people of different racial groups. However, although there is presently no specific EU source for racial equality in the workplace, that is shortly to change for the reasons described elsewhere.

SECTION 2

POSITION POST-HRA

In the employment field, the new rights of relevance available under the HRA are as follows.

Before setting them out, it should be remembered that there is existing case law from the ECommHR and ECtHR on many of these issues. Also, as said above, the primary role of these rights will be to augment existing rights by allowing individuals to raise fresh arguments wherever possible, often combining them with an existing claim under the RRA.

There have already been a number of appeal cases concerning the impact of the HRA in the employment field. However, they have dealt in the main with Tribunal procedures and none as yet have had involved racial discrimination issues. It has recently been confirmed that the Employment Appeals Tribunal does not have the power to make a declaration of incompatibility (see *Whittaker v P & D Watson*, EAT, 07.02.02).

Article 3

Prohibition of Torture

This includes the right not to be subjected to inhuman or degrading treatment or punishment. In this context, consider:

- Extreme forms of workplace racial harassment, such as those involving physical violence. See, for example, the case of *East African Asians v UK* (1973) 3 EHRR 76. Consider also the treatment meted out to Mr Jones in the well-known case of *Jones v Tower Boot Co Ltd* [1997] 2 All ER 406 CA, which might have been sufficiently serious to be covered by Article 3.

Article 4

Prohibition of Slavery and Forced Labour

This includes the right to freedom from forced or compulsory labour. In this context, consider:

- Those from abroad who work in domestic near-servitude, often without a work permit and for long hours and poor pay, and sometimes not allowed to leave the employer's premises;
- Those who have a religious belief preventing work on a particular day of the week, but who are compelled by their employers to work.

Article 6

The Right to a Fair Trial

This includes, in seeking the determination of civil rights and obligations or of any criminal charge, the right to a fair and public hearing within a reasonable time by an independent and impartial tribunal. In this context, consider:

- The lack of legal aid to those who wish to bring complex racial discrimination claims, but do not do so because they cannot afford it. This has already changed in Scotland since the introduction of the HRA, but there are no present plans to introduce legal aid for RRA claims in England and Wales.

Note that Article 6 almost certainly does not cover an employer's internal disciplinary procedures. This is likely still to be the case even with more formal disciplinary procedures such as those within the public service: see the ECtHR case of *Pellegrin v France* (08/12/1999).

Article 8

The Right to Respect for Private and Family Life

This includes the right to respect for one's home and correspondence. In this context, consider:

- The right to ensure that private correspondence through work, by letter, telephone or e-mail, is not vetted by an employer (especially if the employer is attempting to 'eavesdrop' on matters relevant to that employee's racial discrimination claim). The right to privacy will also be relevant when determining an employee's rights under RIPA and the Telecommunications (Lawful Business Practice) (Interception of Communications) Regulations 2000; and
- The adequacy of the RRA governing the liability of employers where racial harassment takes place by co-workers but outside the course of their employment, such as harassment that spills over into home attacks.

Article 9

Freedom of Thought, Conscience and Religion

This includes the right to manifest religion or belief in worship, teaching, practice and observance. In this context, consider:

- The right to have time off for daily worship or religious holidays;
- The right to membership of ethnic-rights organisations.

Article 10

Freedom of Expression
This includes the freedom to hold opinions and to receive and impart information and ideas without interference by public authority. In this context, consider:

- The right to express views at work on ethnic-rights issues without censorship, such as putting up polemical posters;
- By the same token, where the line should be drawn in permitting the dissemination of propaganda or opinions promoting racial supremacy or spreading racial hatred;
- The right to expose racist practices at work, perhaps in contravention of a confidentiality clause in a contract of employment or termination agreement, and not necessarily within the scope of the sections of the ERA dealing with whistleblowing at work;
- The right to dress for work in a manner that may be consistent with religious beliefs but inconsistent with the employer's requirements (such as the wearing of a veil or beard) – see the chapter on religious discrimination for more details;
- The right to criticise an employer over shortcomings in its equal opportunities policies without fear of disciplinary action;
- In the context of victimisation under the RRA, the right to speak out in assisting another employee with a racial discrimination claim.

Article 11

Freedom of Assembly and Association
This includes the right to associate with others, including the right to form and join trade unions. In this context, consider:

- The right of a trade union to consult and bargain on its members' behalf over equal opportunities issues;
- The role of non-trade union organisations, such as ethnic-rights groups, where freedom to associate (at work or elsewhere) is important.

Article 14

Prohibition of Discrimination
The nature of Article 14 has been discussed elsewhere. Article 14 will make

it easier than it has been in the past to complain of racial discrimination by reference to other features not expressly covered by the RRA but which nonetheless can form part of racial identity, such as discrimination by:

- Language (including English spoken with an ethnic accent);
- Religion (including Muslim individuals);
- Association with a national minority (including, for example, Afghan refugees);
- Birth or social origin (school or home address as identified on job application form shown to be in multi-racial area);
- Property (such as style accessories and possessions very popular with particular ethnic groups); and
- 'Other status' (such as appearance, haircut, nose-studs etc).

The Article 14 concept of discrimination does not expressly extend to *indirect* discrimination. There will be different arguments about how such treatment can be justified, which have been set out in the introductory chapter. However, it should be remembered that cases based on similar factual scenarios have been brought under the RRA. Article 14 will be of assistance in augmenting those sorts of claims.

SECTION 3
WHO CAN CLAIM?

As already highlighted in the other chapters, claims under the HRA can be brought by anyone who is (or would be) a victim of an act made unlawful by the HRA. The victim can be any legal entity. In the employment field, this will mostly mean employees. However, it could also mean employers and trade unions.

The HRA contains a new one-year time limit for commencing proceedings, but this is expressly stated to be subject to any shorter time periods that may exist. It does *not* extend the three-month time limit for bringing proceedings under the RRA (or the similar time limit that operates in judicial review cases).

SECTION 4
WHO IS LIABLE?

This section is more complicated than it is in many other chapters in this book. It requires an examination of the circumstances in which employers can be sued under the HRA.

Can human rights claims be brought directly against employers?
This question is essential, because its answer highlights the actual difference the new rights will make in the employment field. Who, at the end of the day, will be liable for breaching the new rights? For example:

- Can an employee whose 'private and confidential' mail is opened by his manager, in the hope of seeing something of relevance to his racial discrimination claim, argue that his *employer* has thereby breached his Article 8 right to privacy?
- Can an employee dismissed for having a political opinion disliked by her employer claim that her *employer* has thereby breached her Article 14 right not to be discriminated against on such a ground?

This issue goes to the heart of the HRA in the employment field. Using the concepts set out in the introduction, will the new human rights have '*horizontal* effect' (allowing employees to claim directly against their employers) or '*vertical* effect' (meaning that employees have no cause of action against their employers, and can only complain against the state for failing to protect those rights)? The answer is: it will depend upon the employer.

Three types of employer
The most important method by which the HRA expands those who can be liable to a claim is to increase the pool of potential respondents from the signatory state itself to all 'public authorities': central and local government, the police, immigration officers, prisons, privatised utilities and the courts and tribunals.

The HRA appears to refer to *three* types of public authority, identified in the introduction as 'pure' public authorities, 'hybrid' public authorities and courts/tribunals. This means that there are three types of employer.

Private sector employers
Private sector companies, such as high street retailers, building societies, law firms and so on, are private bodies with primary duties owed to their shareholders, investors or partners. They carry out acts of an essentially private, not public, nature. They are not public authorities, and so fall outside the scope of the HRA.

Employees of such bodies will *not* be able to claim that their employers have breached their human rights. They can only claim that their human rights have been breached *by the state* for allowing the employer's behaviour to go unpunished by the law (see 'claims against the state' below).

'Pure' public authority employers
Some employers will obviously be public authorities for the purposes of the

HRA (such as local authorities, state schools, the court service, NHS trusts and so on) that they will be liable under the HRA for both their public *and private* acts. As a consequence, the employment relationship, despite being fundamentally private in nature, will be covered by the HRA.

Employees of such bodies will be able to claim *directly* against their employers that their employers have breached their Convention rights.

'Hybrid' public authority employers

Many employers in the public sector will fall between these two extremes. What, for example, is the status of the Post Office, London Underground, Railtrack, British Airways, the BBC, and companies who provided contracted-out services to local authorities and the public schools? These employers are often mixed public-private enterprises.

This third category is described in the HRA as including those bodies that are public authorities because 'certain' of their functions are 'functions of a public nature'. In broad terms, such bodies will only be covered by the HRA for acts done in pursuance of their *public* functions, e.g. providing public transport, or carrying mail. By contrast, where the nature of the act is *private*, it cannot be the subject of a claim under the HRA. As the employment relationship is fundamentally a private one, discipline and dismissal by such an employer will not be actionable under the HRA.

Claims against the state

So, in the employment field, the HRA is of most importance to those working wholly in the public sector. That is not to say that those employed wholly in the private sector or by 'hybrid' public authorities will derive no benefit from the provisions of the HRA. Funding and merits permitting, they may in certain cases be able to take action against the UK in domestic courts for permitting (or failing to prevent) violations of human rights by their employer. The idea is that the state may still be liable for allowing an employer to fail to respect its employees' human rights. In other words, an employee will not complain against his or her *employer*, but against the *state* for allowing the employer to get away with it!

Areas of uncertainty

Until domestic case law has developed, doubts will persist on two central issues:

1. *Where should the line be drawn between 'pure' and 'hybrid' public authorities?*
   Clearly, the answer to this question is very important. It will set out the boundaries for the types of employers that stand to be liable for

breaching the human rights of their employees. The development of case law in this area will be watched with interest.

2. *What is a public or private act?*
    This question will be crucial for determining which acts committed by the 'hybrid' public authorities are actionable. The courts are likely to resolve the matter by reference to existing case law in the context of judicial review proceedings. The courts are well used to the delineation between public and private acts in considering which bodies and actions in the employment field are susceptible to judicial review.

    In *R v East Berkshire Health Authority, ex parte Walsh* [1985] 1 QB 152, the Court of Appeal asserted that 'employment by a public body does not *per se* inject any element of public law and there is no warrant for equating public law with the interest of the public'. By extension, for the HRA to apply between 'hybrid' public authorities (in their capacity as employers) and their employees, it will probably have to be in cases where something *more* than rights based on the contract are at issue.

    This might include rights set out in a policy of more general application, such as a collective agreement or a redundancy policy, which is said to have a discriminatory effect. There is a chance that, in due course, the courts will hear claims by individuals against such 'hybrid' employers based solely on the HRA, where the employee was adversely affected by a flawed decision of general application. In certain cases, the courts may be prepared to accept that the more serious nature of an accusation of an abuse of human rights makes it more susceptible to judicial review. This does leave the door open to limited arguments of 'horizontality' in due course, although it is likely that the courts will be slow to develop them.

The way to complain

It can be seen that the extent to which the HRA may be used in employment litigation depends upon numerous factors, including the nature of the employer whose acts are being challenged (i.e. whether pure, hybrid or neither) and, in certain cases involving hybrid bodies, the nature of the acts under challenge (i.e. whether private or in pursuance of a public function).

An outstanding question to answer is: do Employment Tribunals in any event have jurisdiction to hear such claims? Where a cause of action against a public authority is created by the HRA, s.7(1)(a) provides that proceedings may only be brought in the 'appropriate court or tribunal'. The question can therefore be re-phrased thus: are Employment Tribunals 'appropriate' for these purposes?

As creatures of statute, Tribunals require that an applicant must identify a statutory provision that confers jurisdiction on them. There are as yet no statutory rules confirming jurisdiction on Employment Tribunals to hear cases against pure public authorities. This is unfortunate as it means that applicants with human rights issues will have to go through the separate civil court system, where the costs rules are different (as separately explained in the chapter on funding).

It follows that, for the moment, the most appropriate fora for enforcing freestanding actions to enforce the new rights created by the HRA are the County Court and the High Court. In fact, the High Court will be the only appropriate forum where the proceedings involve an application for judicial review or an attempt to obtain a declaration of incompatibility. This will be true:

- For all pure public authorities; and
- For all hybrid public authorities, to the extent that the acts under challenge are those in pursuance of their public functions (which itself may depend upon development of arguments over the public v. private divide).

Accordingly, a s.7(1)(a) action by an employee against a pure public authority employer for breach of a Convention right will usually be taken in the County Court or High Court. (There are specific exceptions to this; in certain circumstances, claims involving alleged breaches of Article 8 can only be brought before the RIPA Tribunal). An applicant cannot plead 'breach of the HRA' in his or her application to the Tribunal, because the Tribunal has no jurisdiction to hear such a claim.

In a Tribunal case involving legislation over which the Tribunal already has jurisdiction, an applicant can invite the Tribunal to have regard to any relevant Strasbourg case law and read that legislation in a manner compatible with the Convention. Although this does not mean that the applicant has invoked any cause of action under the HRA, it means the Tribunal can give still effect to the Convention in a more subtle way.

It follows that, where an applicant wishes to rely on the Convention in Tribunal proceedings, he or she must identify an existing claim (in respect of which the Tribunal already has jurisdiction) on which to 'hang' the Convention argument, e.g. unfair dismissal under the ERA, or discrimination prohibited by the SDA, RRA or DDA.

Indeed, this is currently the *only* avenue for raising Convention arguments in cases against hybrid public authority employers and private sector employers. That argument can then be used to persuade the Tribunal to determine the existing claim by reading the legislation over which it *does* have jurisdiction in a manner compatible with the Convention. Readers will be forgiven for wanting a wet towel around their heads when reading this part of the employment chapter again!

Practical features

Many practical matters are dealt with more fully elsewhere in this book, but those of particular relevance to employment law are as follows.

1. Always look for the human rights angle in connection with racial discrimination, especially in the context of Article 14.
2. Think laterally in looking for Article 14 features that, while not obviously racial, have a racial element – accent, social origin, religion, appearance. If referring to Article 14, always remember to identify the other Convention right that is also allegedly being breached.
3. Do not forget the three-month time limits for bringing racial discrimination claims. This time limit will not be extended simply because there is a human rights issue involved.
4. Consider contacting the organisations identified in the 'useful addresses' section at the end. Can they be of assistance in providing funding?
5. Identify at the outset of a claim into which of the three categories the employer in question falls. If it is a private sector employer, investigate whether there is any feature of the case suggesting that the RRA is lacking in protecting the human rights of your client at work. If it is a 'hybrid' employer, investigate whether there is any argument that the human rights breach committed by your client's employer constitutes a 'public act', so that a claim could be brought against the employer direct.
6. Make sure that any claim is brought in the correct forum.

SECTION 5

Case Study

Mr Hussein, a Muslim employee, requests time off during work to attend to daily prayers, but his employer refuses on account of being short-staffed and requiring high productivity. He takes the time off anyway and, following an investigation and disciplinary hearing, he is dismissed for gross misconduct. It might be said that his dismissal was contrary to Articles 9 and 14 (freedom to manifest religious belief and non-discrimination on grounds of religion).

To which forum should Mr Hussein complain? Regardless of the nature of his employer (pure, hybrid or private), he can already proceed to an Employment Tribunal in an action for unfair dismissal under the ERA. He could seek to rely on the RRA, but such a claim would probably fail because Muslims are not a racial or national group under the RRA and discrimination in employment on the grounds of religious belief will not be prohibited in mainland Britain until the Employment Equality (Religion or Belief) Regulations 2003 – currently in draft form – come into force.

What difference has the HRA made? In the unfair dismissal case, Mr Hussein could ask the Tribunal to read the ERA in a manner compatible with the Convention so that, having regard to the equity and substantial merits of the case, it could not find that the employer acted reasonably under s.98(4) ERA; hence, the dismissal must be unfair. In the race discrimination case, he could ask the Tribunal to read words into the RRA so that it does in fact prohibit discrimination against him on religious grounds, but the prospects of such an argument succeeding are greatly in doubt. Certainly, a post-HRA attempt to read the word 'sex' in the SDA as extending to sexual orientation has already been unsuccessful.

It is only if Mr Hussein's employer was a pure public authority that he could claim that his employer had acted unlawfully under the Convention, and therefore bring a freestanding claim under Article 9, possibly in conjunction with Article 14. Such proceedings would not be brought in the Employment Tribunal for the reasons identified above. It is currently unclear whether, in such circumstances, Mr Hussein should proceed first to the ordinary civil courts, followed by the Tribunal, or vice versa, or the extent to which one set of proceedings should be stayed while the other progressed. This is likely to be a decision made on the facts of each case in view of the remedy available.

The remedy available will also be critical in determining the choice of forum. For example, a pre-dismissal injunction could be sought from the civil courts, although these are granted only in exceptional circumstances. Also, a strong complaint of unfair dismissal that may be pursued more cheaply in the Tribunal might well be more cost-effective than an expensive civil court action for an alleged breach of human rights. It is appropriate to question the cost-effectiveness of separate proceedings involving an alleged breach of human rights if the individual complainant is likely to receive a quicker and more effective remedy from the Tribunal.

Finding legal assistance for racial discrimination cases

Helena Cook

INTRODUCTION

It can be a tough challenge for a victim of racial discrimination to find good and affordable legal advice. As the above chapters have demonstrated, racial discrimination is a specialised area of law and there are relatively few practitioners and advice agencies out there with expertise in this field. The HRA (and increasingly EC law) brings in other complex and specialised areas and, as this book has shown, will enable discrimination issues to be raised in a wide variety of other legal proceedings.

There are statutory bodies with specific responsibility for monitoring the implementation of anti-discrimination legislation: the Commission for Racial Equality, the Equal Opportunities Commission and the Disability Rights Commission. However, so far the government has resisted calls to establish a similar body to oversee cases brought under the HRA. However, with the recent consultation paper 'Equality and Diversity: Making It Happen', the Government has indicated a potential willingness to create a single equal opportunities body, incorporating not only race, sex and disability, but also new equality areas such as religion, belief, sexual orientation and, at some stage in the future, age. The present thinking is that any such institution is unlikely to come into being until 2006. Nevertheless, it may still prove difficult to develop a consistent body of human rights case law, while human rights is seen to remain outside the equality framework.

Legal advisers should be able to give realistic and holistic advice to enable a potential client to explore a range of possible options, including but certainly not limited to legal action in the courts. Legal proceedings can be prolonged, expensive and very stressful and may not be the best way to resolve a problem. Racial discrimination cases are hard to win and do not tend to deliver high levels of compensation. A person may anyway have other compelling motives for taking action that have little to do with money and it needs to be explored whether litigation is the best way to deliver these desired results.

There is an increasing awareness of racial discrimination and allegations are being taken more seriously. The law is developing and becoming more complex. At the same time, racial discrimination is often difficult to prove and cases need a lot of careful and detailed preparation if they are to succeed. Tribunal hearings are taking longer and are no longer simple and informal. Private legal assistance is not cheap and the cost of legal proceedings can mount up alarmingly relative to the levels of compensation that can be expected in most cases.

In an Employment Tribunal case where there has been real financial loss, such as lost earnings after a person has lost their job, damages may reach significant figures. However, many discrimination cases do not involve much, if any, financial loss. The chapter on employment has given some indication of average figures, but it cannot be stressed enough that strong evidence of serious physical harassment and deeply offensive language and behaviour are required before damages are pushed up even as high as £10,000. Costs, on the other hand, can range from between a few thousand pounds (cheaper if the case is settled quickly) to many tens of thousands of pounds. The longer the hearing, the higher the cost. In High Court proceedings, such as judicial review, which are likely to be more widely used for human rights cases, a full hearing can easily incur costs of £10,000 and will rise to a lot more in a more complicated case that runs for several days.

In Employment Tribunal cases successful complainants do not recover their own costs, although equally they do not have to pay the other side's costs if they lose. In High Court or County Court proceedings, successful complainants can generally recover their own costs but, if they lose, will usually have to pay the costs of the other side as well.

There is very little public funding (what used to be called legal aid) available for discrimination cases, partly because the stringent financial eligibility rules exclude all but the poorest complainant and partly because there is no public funding for Employment Tribunal cases. There are some other free or low-cost sources of legal advice but these are not enough to meet demand, may be of variable quality and are certainly not evenly spread or accessible throughout the country.

This chapter looks at various possible sources of legal assistance for racial discrimination cases and how to access these. Full contact details for all the organisations referred to can be found in the list of useful names, addresses and websites at the end of this chapter.

THE COMMUNITY LEGAL SERVICE

The Community Legal Service was launched by the government in April

2000 as a new initiative to improve access to all kinds of legal assistance. It aims to provide a network of legal services that meet a recognised standard of quality. Local authorities, solicitors and advice agencies are being encouraged to set up local Community Legal Service Partnerships and to establish comprehensive referral networks so that people are directed quickly and efficiently to the best source of legal help for their problem.

The Community Legal Service is principally aimed at people who need low-cost or free legal assistance. It is being developed alongside a major reform of the legal aid scheme. Although the Community Legal Service encompasses all solicitors and legal advisers able to do legal aid work under the new scheme, it is much broader than this and it is by no means restricted only to people who would qualify for legal aid. Anyone who has a legal problem can tap into the Community Legal Service for assistance. The CLS includes agencies that can offer low-cost or free assistance as well as private solicitors who charge fees for their services. It is up to the individual to use the Community Legal Service resources and structures to find the source of legal assistance best suited to their problem and their pocket.

Community Legal Service providers will display the CLS logo indicating that they have passed the necessary quality checks. They will fall within one of two main categories: information services and help services. Those that offer 'information' only will essentially signpost someone to the most appropriate source of legal assistance. Those that offer 'help' should be able to identify the key elements of a problem and provide advice on action to be taken. There are different levels of 'help', both general (such as Citizens Advice Bureaux) and specialist (such as a Law Centre or solicitor with expertise in certain areas of law and carrying out a full range of legal services including representation at court).

There are 13 Community Legal Service Regional Directories covering North London, South London, Southern, South Eastern, South West, West Midlands, North West, North East, Yorkshire and Humberside, East Midlands, East, Wales and Merseyside. The CLS Directories are kept by solicitors, advice agencies, local authorities and local information points such as public libraries. An electronic version is available on the CLS website. They can also be purchased from the Resource Information Service. They list legal services providers town by town in the region and have an alphabetical index of provider names and an index by category of law. Each entry gives details of the provider, including specialist expertise, hours of opening and fees and charging arrangements.

The Community Legal Service is very much in its infancy and is still being developed. The early versions of the Directories have been criticised for errors and, until April 2002, they will include providers who have yet to achieve the quality standards. The latest Directories do have a separate category for 'racial equality' indicating providers with some expertise in this area, but not yet for the human rights/civil liberties category of law. For a racial discrimination problem it may also be worth searching for providers in related areas relevant to the problem such as employment, education, immigration, consumer and general contract, housing or public law. However, there is no guarantee that these providers would be best placed to take on a racial discrimination case. Still the CLS could be a useful starting point to locate local legal services. It is likely to become more useful as time goes on and it becomes better developed and organised and more widely known.

LEGAL AID

The government has recently undertaken a major reform of the legal aid scheme and has re-named or replaced all the old structures and systems. The Legal Services Commission has replaced the old Legal Aid Board and administers two new public funding schemes.

The pot of money for legal assistance in civil and family cases is known as the Community Legal Service Fund, launched in April 2000. A year later, the government launched a second public funding scheme for criminal cases, the Criminal Defence Service (replacing Criminal Legal Aid). There are specific eligibility rules for public funding for defendants in criminal cases. Although, as the chapter on criminal law indicates, racial discrimination issues under the HRA may well arise in criminal cases, this section concentrates on the availability of public funding for civil cases only.

Public funding can now only be obtained through a solicitor or advice agency that has a contract with the Legal Services Commission. Only Community Legal Service quality marked organisations at the specialist level are eligible for contracts. Lists of these firms and agencies, which will display the new CLS logo, can be found in the Community Legal Service Directories (see above).

Financial eligibility

To qualify for public funding a person must first be eligible under the very strict financial limits. These are calculated differently for the different types of assistance explained below. A solicitor or advice agency will be able to advise someone whether or not he or she qualifies for public funds. The following information is included as a rough guide only as the eligibility conditions change periodically.

Capital and income are taken into account after various deductions for dependants, national insurance, tax, rent, rates and other necessary expenses. What is left is called 'disposable' capital and income. The value of the person's house is included although any equity below a certain level, after allowing a maximum deduction for a mortgage, is excluded. Certain welfare benefits are excluded from income. If the person is married or has a live-in partner then his or her capital and income will also usually be taken into account.

Levels of assistance

The different levels of civil legal assistance most relevant in racial discrimination cases are as follows.

Legal help

This covers initial advice and assistance with a potential case from a solicitor or other organisation providing legal services (formerly known as the 'Green Form Scheme'). It can include writing letters, advice about how the law applies, help in settling or resolving a dispute, getting a barrister's opinion and so on. Initially, two hours of Legal Help can be given, but this can be extended if necessary to complete the work.

In addition to financial eligibility, Legal Help can only be provided if two basic criteria are met: there must be a 'sufficient benefit' to the client to justify the work; and it must be 'reasonable' for the work to be publicly funded.

Legal representation

This covers legal assistance and services for all the work leading up to and including representation by a solicitor or barrister in civil court proceedings. In racial discrimination cases, public funding for legal representation is available for cases in the County Court, judicial review proceedings in the High Court and proceedings before Immigration Adjudicators and the Immigration Appeals Tribunal (but *not* for cases before an Employment Tribunal).

In order to qualify for funding for legal representation certain criteria have to be met and a detailed cost benefits test is applied:

- The prospects of success must be at least 50% or more;
- If the prospects of success are 50%-60%, likely damages must exceed likely costs by 4:1; if the prospects of success are 60%-80%, likely damages must exceed likely costs by 2:1; if the prospects of success are 80% or more, likely damages must simply exceed likely costs;
- If the claim is not primarily a claim for damages, likely benefits must justify likely costs such that a reasonable private paying client would be prepared to litigate;

- If the case is suitable for a Conditional Fee Agreement and the client is likely to be able to obtain one, funding will be refused (see below);
- There must be no sources of alternative funding or others who could reasonably bring or fund the case;
- There must be no complaints systems or alternative forms of dispute resolution that should be tried before litigation;
- It must not be unreasonable for the Legal Services Commission to fund representation.

Investigative help

This is a preliminary form of Legal Representation to enable investigation of the strength of a proposed claim. It can include initial steps in issuing and conducting legal proceedings in order to obtain information or to protect the client's position. To obtain funds for investigation there must be reasonable grounds to believe that the claim will be strong enough to justify full representation in due course and, if the claim is for damages, the likely damages must exceed £5,000.

Once the HRA is in force, it is likely that racial discrimination issues will be more frequently litigated in High Court proceedings against public authorities. In these proceedings, the cost benefits test is not so strict and requires only that the likely benefits must justify the costs.

Public interest and human rights cases

There are special rules for the public funding of cases with a significant wider public interest or raising significant human rights issues. This should mean that these cases have a better chance of securing public funding (provided the client meets the financial eligibility tests). Some racial discrimination cases, particularly those raising issues under the HRA, may well qualify for inclusion in these special categories.

A case with a significant wider public interest is one with the potential to produce real benefits (not only financial but also less quantifiable benefits such as the protection of rights, health, safety and quality of life) for a group of individuals – probably at least 100 others or many more if the benefits are general and intangible. Such a case may be funded even if the prospects of success are borderline and a looser cost benefits test is applied rather than the very strict ratios of costs to damages outlined above.

Cases raising significant human rights issues are those where the human rights issues are an important part of the case, have a reasonable prospect of success and are likely to make a difference to the outcome. Such cases have been designated a priority for public funding and can be funded even if the prospects of success are borderline. Weight will also be given to the human rights issues in applying the cost benefit test.

There is also a presumption that public funding *will* be granted for judicial review proceedings which fall into these categories (once the court has granted leave to proceed), regardless of the prospects of success and the cost benefit analysis.

These rules on public interest and human rights are still relatively new, so it remains hard to predict how they will work in practice and what sort of cases may qualify. But they may be well worth considering in suitable racial discrimination cases. The Legal Services Commission has even set up a Public Interest Advisory Panel to assist its Regional Offices in decisions as to whether a case has a wider public interest element. The Panel comprises two Commission members and representatives from the Consumers Association, the Law Society, the Bar Council and the non-governmental organisations Liberty, Justice and the Public Law Project.

TRADE UNIONS

If a person is a member of a trade union and the racial discrimination case arises in the context of employment, then legal advice and representation may well be available through the union. Some union legal protection plans may even extend to cover cases arising outside the employment context. Most providers of legal advice will urge an individual first to seek help from their union (if he or she is a member). It is always worth exploring this option at the outset.

The elimination of discrimination of all kinds is generally a priority issue for trade unions and there should be well-established and well-publicised procedures to follow in the event of a potential complaint. Applications for assistance usually have to be made through local branch and/or regional union officials. Alternatively there may be designated officials with specific responsibility for racial or discrimination issues. A few unions have full in-house legal departments that not only advise and represent claimants before Tribunals but which say they can offer a more holistic service, with recourse to other possible courses of union action short of legal proceedings. Other unions will contract litigation out to private solicitors. Unions will generally want to consider the strength of the claim and the likely cost of proceedings, among other factors, before deciding whether to proceed. Some unions are more flexible than others and claim, for example, to take on all well-founded complaints, regardless of cost.

Unions do provide a significant source of free legal assistance – at least in employment cases – and may give some victims of discrimination their only chance of pursuing a case. However, there are many complaints about union representation and a widely held perception that much more needs to be done by unions to provide meaningful and effective legal advice and assistance schemes. For example, difficulties may be encountered if the person complained against is also a union member and the union does not want to institute legal proceedings; if the union pushes other forms of dispute resolution rather than litigation against the claimant's wishes; if the front-line officials do not fully understand the issues and block access to legal advice at a higher or more specialised level; if the union and the complainant disagree at any point as to how to proceed; or if the union initially takes up a case but later refuses to continue.

The Trades Union Congress has a useful leaflet on racism at work and publishes a guide to union action for race equality. It also runs a TUC Know Your Rights telephone line that may be helpful if difficulties are encountered in getting a union to take up a case or if there is no union at the workplace.

THE COMMISSION FOR RACIAL EQUALITY

The Commission for Racial Equality is a non-governmental publicly funded body set up under the RRA to oversee its implementation and to tackle racial discrimination and promote racial equality. It has the capacity to assist and represent individual complainants in legal action against racial discrimination. As stated above, it is possible that, at some stage (probably 2006 at the earliest), the CRE may fall under an umbrella equalities body.

Since the CRE is a statutory body, it has to take up cases within the framework of the RRA and this may limit its scope of action under the HRA (it has requested that its statutory competence be formally extended to include the HRA but this has not been agreed). However, the CRE will not be ignoring the human rights dimension. Human rights arguments will still be relevant in many RRA cases.

The CRE considers all applications for assistance but receives many more requests than it actually takes up. According to the CRE, this is more often due to the weaknesses of the cases submitted to it rather than scarcity of resources. In 1999, for example, it received a total of 1,624 applications for assistance but only gave representation in 304 cases (18%).

The RRA lays down three criteria that the CRE must use to decide which cases to support: cases that test a point of law; cases that are too complex for an individual to deal with alone; and cases that deserve special consideration. In practice, these are applied fairly flexibly and one of the primary considerations is the merits of the case, among other factors. The CRE also expects applicants to try any alternative sources of assistance first, such as a trade union or public funding from the Community Legal Service Fund.

Once an application is received by the CRE it is examined by a complaints officer who will assist in the preliminary groundwork to prepare the case. However, this does not indicate that the CRE has agreed to act. The final decision on which cases to support is made by the CRE's Legal Committee (made up of CRE Commissioners who are not necessarily legally qualified). The Committee decides whether legal assistance can be offered and, if so, to what level. If there are questions about the case, for example, the CRE may initially agree to fund only a legal opinion from a barrister in order to decide whether or not to proceed.

Once a case is accepted for legal representation, the applicant must voluntarily concede to hand over much of the decision-making in relation to the case. The CRE decides how to conduct the case, nominates legal representatives, deals with the media if necessary and reserves the right to withdraw representation at any time, such as if a reasonable offer to settle is made but not accepted.

Anyone who wants to approach the CRE to apply for legal assistance in a racial discrimination case must obtain and fill in an application form providing all the relevant information. The form and further information can be obtained from the CRE or downloaded from the internet. It is important to act promptly because of the tight time limits for discrimination cases and the fact that it can take two to four months for the CRE to make its decision about whether or not to provide representation.

RACIAL EQUALITY COUNCILS

There are over 100 Racial Equality Councils (RECs) throughout the country. They are part-funded by the CRE to fulfil similar functions at a local level of promoting racial equality and tackling discrimination. Historically, there has been an expectation by the CRE that all RECs should spend a certain proportion of their time on assisting individual complainants, including providing Tribunal representation. In practice this has not happened and the quality and quantity of complainant aid work varies enormously between RECs. Only a very few, it seems, actually do provide Tribunal representation.

However, all RECs should, at the very least, be able to give people some initial advice about a possible discrimination case and sign-post people on to more specialist sources of legal advice such as the CRE, a local Law Centre, other advice agencies or private solicitors. A case that is well prepared by a good REC may have a much better chance of acceptance for representation by the CRE, for example. A few of the RECs are, however, very experienced and can offer good legal advice and assistance in individual cases, including representation before Employment Tribunals. Their services are free but they may actively seek voluntary contributions if a case is successful. Since REC officers are mostly not legally qualified, they are not generally able to provide representation in the High Court or County Court.

Most RECs have quite limited staff and resources and suffer from a lack of support and training other than what they can arrange and fund for themselves locally. It is likely to take quite some time before most of them develop any expertise on the HRA and are in a position to offer good legal advice on possible discrimination issues arising under it.

RECs can be located via the telephone directory, local libraries, from local authority information sources or from the CRE itself. Some have their own websites on the Internet.

LAW CENTRES

Law Centres are voluntary organisations employing solicitors and some-times barristers. There are currently 51 Law Centres in England and Wales (23 are based in London), grouped under a national body, the Law Centres Federation, which publishes a full listing. They generally offer legal advice and representation to clients within their catchment area on a range of social welfare law and related issues, including discrimination, although some will have particular specialisations. They work closely with local Citizens Advice Bureaux and other advice agencies. Their services are free but increasingly Law Centres are becoming more dependent on public funding from the Legal Services Commission that can only be used for clients who qualify for such assistance.

The London Race Discrimination Unit – North Lambeth Law Centre
This is a relatively new Unit, funded by the CRE, to provide free advice and representation to clients living or working in London who have experienced race discrimination in the workplace. It is working in partnership with a leading set of barristers' chambers that will provide free representation in courts and Tribunals. It also aims to set up a duty solicitor scheme in the London Employment Tribunals and to establish a special support group for claimants bringing proceedings against employers where discrimination is institutionalised.

The Bristol and Avon Law Centre
This Law Centre is part-funded by the CRE to provide a specialist service of free legal assistance and representation in all racial discrimination cases.

Its remit extends to the counties of the South West of England. It works closely with the Bristol Racial Equality Council.

ADVICE AGENCIES AND OTHER ORGANISATIONS

Local advice agencies are another valuable source of free or low-cost legal assistance. Some may offer no more than sign-posting to specialist legal advice while others will be able to offer advice and assistance themselves and even, depending on their resources, full legal representation. They should be able to be located through local libraries, telephone directories, local authority information points, the Community Legal Service Directories and so on, although it may be difficult in an initial trawl to identify those with any expertise in discrimination work. Also brand new specialist areas of law, like the HRA, can present a difficult challenge for advice agencies with few resources and limited access to training. It may be a while before some agencies feel confident to offer advice and assistance in the new area of human rights law.

Citizens Advice Bureaux
CABx are perhaps the best known of the advice agencies. Their services are free and they should be able to provide basic advice and information on a discrimination case and, as appropriate, signpost a client on to more specialised sources of help. Depending on their own staffing and resources, they may be able to provide specialist help themselves, including some legal representation. Many CABx have formalised referral arrangements with local solicitors and a high proportion benefit from the services of a rota of volunteer solicitors who attend advice sessions. There is now a CAB Advice Guide on the internet that is easy to use and enables individuals to access basic advice on a range of different topics, including discrimination. It also has contact details for all CABx.

The Northern Complainants Aid Fund
This is an organisation funded by the CRE to provide free legal assistance in racial discrimination cases to people who would otherwise be without help. Its advisers are not legally qualified solicitors but are themselves former complainants who have some first-hand experience of discrimination. It acts only in employment cases and can assist people with cases in the Employment Tribunals. Court proceedings will require a solicitor. The remit of the West Yorkshire office covers the whole of the north of England, while the office recently established in Birmingham serves the Midlands.

Liberty

This is a well-known civil liberties and human rights organisation that undertakes test case litigation, lobbying, campaigning and research. It has prioritised discrimination as one of four areas for work under the HRA and is particularly interested in racism in the context of the criminal justice system. Its in-house legal staff will take up individual cases free of charge. However, it very carefully selects those cases that it takes on and, inevitably, these are only a fraction of the total number of inquiries it receives. Individuals should send full details of their case to the Advice and Information Officer. There is also an Advice Line with telephone advice and referrals provided by qualified solicitors and barristers. Jointly with the Public Law Project, Liberty also runs a free telephone consultancy service in public law and human rights for lawyers and advisers who hold a contract from the Legal Services Commission.

The Public Law Project

This is an organisation that seeks to improve access to public law remedies for the disadvantaged. It conducts casework and litigation in a small number of test cases as well as undertaking research and training and acting as a specialist public law resource for other lawyers and advice agencies. It has particular expertise in judicial review and, with the entry into force of the HRA, expects discrimination issues to feature more prominently in its work. It has a general public law Advice Line as well as the Human Rights Consultancy run jointly with Liberty (see above).

The Aire Centre

This does not litigate cases in the UK courts but can provide expert advice and assistance on all matters relating to the Convention, including discrimination, to lawyers, advisers and others.

PRO BONO SCHEMES

The phrase 'pro bono' is adapted from the Latin 'pro bono publico', meaning 'for the public good'. Now it tends simply to mean 'free of charge'. The legal profession has always carried out pro bono work, but it has not always been effectively publicised.

The Bar Pro Bono Unit

The Bar Pro Bono Unit was established in 1996 to provide free legal advice and representation for individuals ineligible for public funding but otherwise unable to afford legal assistance. The Pro Bono Panel consists of over

1,000 barristers covering the full range of legal specialisations, including discrimination. These barristers can either give advice in a written opinion or in conference and/or they can provide free legal representation in a court or tribunal. However, each Panel member is only committed to offer up to three pro bono days per year so that it may well be difficult to find barristers on the Panel willing and able to offer significantly more time, for example to cover a complex or lengthy discrimination hearing with a large number of witnesses. On the other hand, the Unit indicates that on occasions in the past Panel members have provided considerably more than the minimum three days when necessary.

This option is also not at all suitable where a great deal of ground work needs to be done on the case, such as gathering evidence, interviewing witnesses, sending correspondence; barristers do not take on this kind of preparatory work. Wherever possible, an application for the services of a barrister under this scheme should be made with the assistance of a solicitor or advice agency caseworker who will continue to work on the case. Otherwise the Unit will assess whether a solicitor is needed, but it is only in exceptional cases that it may be able to find a solicitor willing and able to take on the case without payment.

Applicants must fully complete an application form and send all relevant documents. Decisions as to whether or not the Unit will accept a case are made by members of the Management Committee taking into account the legal merits of the case and the financial circumstances of the applicant, including the possibility of any alternative sources of funding. The Unit does not provide any details about how financial eligibility is approached – only that the individual must demonstrate that he or she is unable to afford legal assistance privately. A decision is generally made within two weeks and the Unit stresses that it cannot guarantee to respond to a more urgent request. If the case is accepted, the Unit informs the applicant of the barrister allocated to the case and how contact will be made. After that, the applicant or his or her solicitor will deal with the barrister directly. The list of barristers on the Panel is not made public and an applicant cannot choose between them.

Solicitors' Pro Bono Group
The Solicitors' Pro Bono Group is not an equivalent to the Bar Pro Bono Unit. It is a membership organisation that aims to support and promote pro bono activities by solicitors. It does not take on pro bono cases itself and is not able to match requests for assistance with solicitors willing to provide free legal advice.

Free Representation Unit

The Free Representation Unit, usually know as 'FRU', has been going for over 25 years. It aims to find volunteer lawyers, both solicitors and barristers, to represent clients before Tribunals – principally in the field of employment and social security. It does not deal directly with members of the public, although it will try to steer those who arrive on its doorstep in the right direction. Instead it operates as a 'second-tier' agency, accepting referrals only from recognised front-line advice agencies such as Citizens Advice Bureaux.

FRU produces a referral guide and standard referral forms need to be completed for each case. Cases are registered and then reviewed by a caseworker to determine what level of legal expertise is needed. Only cases with a hearing date are accepted. FRU does not itself allocate cases – it is up to its members to decide which cases they are willing and able to take on. Once a FRU volunteer accepts a case he or she contacts the client and the referral agency and handles the case as though it were an ordinary private brief.

FRU cannot guarantee to provide representation – there are far more demands for its services than it can meet from its pool of volunteers. Also many of its volunteers are students, pupil barristers, trainee solicitors or those in the very early stages of practice, although all are required to undergo some specialist training. Any referral agency should bear this in mind, particularly in a specialist area such as racial discrimination.

SOLICITORS IN PRIVATE PRACTICE

For those able to contemplate paying legal fees, the first step is to locate a solicitor with the required expertise in racial discrimination and human rights law. Discrimination is a relatively small and specialised area of work for the legal profession and it is not very easy to obtain comprehensive listings of who does what. When consulting any kind of index or listing, if there is no specific entry for race issues or discrimination generally, which is likely, it is worth checking under related relevant categories such as 'Employment', 'General Contract', 'Human Rights' and 'Civil Liberties'. It is important, too, to be aware of the specialisations of solicitors even within the discrimination field. Some will work only in the employment field while others will take on discrimination work across the board; some will have an added expertise already in civil liberties and human rights; some will work exclusively for trade unions; and very few will work only on behalf of individual complainants.

One of the leading directories of the legal profession is the Chambers &

Partners' Directory, which is updated annually and covers both solicitors and barristers. It is not a comprehensive listing but selects firms or chambers with an acknowledged reputation for being the leading specialists in particular fields. It gives information and contact details not only about the firms but also highlights particular individuals within them and includes their personal profiles. It has no specific listing for 'discrimination' but information about discrimination practitioners can be found in other sections such as those on employment and civil liberties. The Directory should be available in law libraries and legal bookshops and may also be found in other main public libraries.

The Discrimination Law Association is a professional grouping of lawyers and advisers practising in the area of discrimination law. Its Directory of members, updated every six months, is available to the public. After the Chambers Directory, it is probably one of the best places to start locating a suitable solicitor for a racial discrimination case. As noted above, the Community Legal Service Directories may also be a useful source for local solicitors, particularly those with a contract to do publicly funded work.

The Employment Lawyers Association, the professional grouping of lawyers specialised in employment law, may also be a useful starting point to find a suitable solicitor to take on a racial discrimination issue arising in the workplace.

The Law Society produces a Directory of Solicitors via the Internet. This is a listing of all its members, their areas of work and their contact details. It will not be available in hard copy. Otherwise, those who approach the Law Society are often simply given 'a couple of names' of solicitors practising in the area inquired about. It is not clear how these names are selected and it is not to be recommended as a good way to locate the best private practitioner for a particular problem.

Potential clients are entitled to expect that solicitors will always explore various funding options with them before going ahead and that they are absolutely clear about the fee arrangements for any legal work undertaken. Some may give a short initial interview free of charge to determine the level and nature of legal assistance required. In some cases relatively new funding options such as conditional fee arrangements and legal expenses insurance may be useful.

Conditional and Contingency Fee Arrangements

In a conditional fee arrangement (CFA), sometimes rather misleadingly called 'no win no fee' arrangements, a solicitor charges his or her normal fees if the case is won, usually with an additional 'success fee' on top. The success fee will be a percentage of the basic costs up to a maximum of

100%. If the case is lost there will be a reduced fee or no fee at all (although in the County or High Court the client is still likely to have to pay the other side's costs). Many barristers' chambers are now geared up to undertake work on CFAs as well.

In all cases it will usually be necessary to pay the incidental expenses such as court fees. These fee arrangements are strictly regulated by law in order to ensure that clients know exactly what they will be charged and in what circumstances. The Law Society provides a model Conditional Fee Arrangement and also has an explanatory leaflet for clients.

In contingency fee arrangements, which are not regulated in the same way as conditional fees, the solicitor's fees are calculated as a percentage of any compensation recovered. These arrangements cannot be used in High Court and County Court cases although, rather incongruously, they are permissible in Employment Tribunal cases.

It is possible to get 'after the event' legal expenses insurance (or 'AEI') policies (to provide cover once a legal claim has arisen) that are specifically linked to a conditional fee agreement. These policies are designed to kick in if the case is lost and the client is liable for the opponent's costs. They generally cover the other side's costs, incidental expenses and the client's own barrister's fees (the expectation being that under the CFA no fees will be payable to the client's own solicitor). They really only make sense for cases in the High Court or County Court, and not for those in Employment Tribunals where the losing party is not liable for the opponent's costs. The insurance market in such products is still in an early stage of development and it is difficult to give a useful indication of what AEI policies may cost.

The difficulty with conditional fee arrangements is that they are rarely economically viable in racial discrimination cases. First, the chances of success tend to be low because racial discrimination is so difficult to prove. The risk of failure may be too great for a solicitor to enter into a conditional fee arrangement. Secondly, even if an Employment Tribunal case is won, the client's legal costs cannot generally be recovered from the losing party. Thirdly, the damages recovered relative to the costs of running the case tend not to be sufficiently high to make these kinds of fee arrangements worthwhile.

Legal expenses insurance

A number of standard household and motoring insurance schemes include a certain level of protection against legal expenses. They only cover legal claims arising after the policy is taken out. For example, a number of the larger insurance companies provide cover of up to £25,000 or £50,000 of legal costs for an additional annual premium of between £10 to £20. Such legal expenses insurance policies are available before the claim has arisen and, in contrast to the above, are sometimes called 'before the event' insurance (or 'BEI') policies.

It is always worth checking the terms of any existing insurance policies to see what may be covered as regards legal fees in connection with complaints of racial discrimination. Indeed, before recommending a conditional fee agreement, with the associated cost of an AEI policy, a solicitor should investigate whether BEI cover is available. Although such policies are rarely aimed at racial discrimination claims (although many cover employment and contractual disputes) their terms will often be broad enough to cover the costs of legal advice and representation in a discrimination case.

Some insurance companies offer AEI policies even when there is no conditional fee arrangement in place. Solicitors should have details of these. These policies are only offered if the insurer thinks there is a good chance of success. Also the premiums tend to be very expensive as, unlike under a CFA, the policy has to cover the client's own legal costs if they lose.

One problem with legal expenses insurance is that insurance companies have little or no knowledge of discrimination law and their products are not really geared for such cases. Some insurers will charge an assessment fee to consider the case and may require a barrister's opinion before offering cover. They will be looking for a good chance of success before agreeing to back a case, which is often very difficult to predict in racial discrimination actions. They may try to insist on their choice of solicitor who may not be a discrimination specialist and their agreement may be needed to engage a barrister or expert witness. If the case does not progress as expected, the insurer may insist on settlement or withdraw cover.

LITIGANTS IN PERSON

Some determined claimants may decide to do their own legal work and to represent themselves in a tribunal or a court. This can be a daunting prospect and is not really to be recommended. Many of the earlier chapters in this book stress the complexity of this field of law and the need for specialist legal advice, particularly with the advent of the new human rights law. As has been stated on numerous occasions, racial discrimination cases are often factually and legally complex and difficult to prove. It can be very hard to obtain the necessary evidence. Witnesses need to be carefully and skilfully examined or cross-examined. There are also strict time limits and special court procedures that must be observed.

Research has repeatedly demonstrated that the chances of success are far less for litigants without legal representation. The other side in the case, which may be an employer, an educational institution, a public body or some other provider of services, is likely to have full legal representation with both a firm of solicitors and a retained barrister, so that the proceedings will start off weighted against the unrepresented litigant. Employment Tribunals are meant to be less formal and more 'user-friendly', and under the HRA they must themselves ensure 'equality of arms' so as to ensure that the parties receive a fair determination of their civil rights under Article 6 of the Convention. However, in practice the assistance they offer is variable and tends to be quite limited.

There is very little assistance available to litigants in person to help them prepare a case and to advise them as to what will happen at the court or tribunal. There is a Litigants in Person Society that may be worth contacting. The Court Service and Tribunals produce some leaflets on their procedures that should be on display on court premises or on request. Some CABx hold periodic advice sessions in the courts and in London there is a CAB office located in the Royal Courts of Justice in the Strand, although these services tend to be very over-stretched.

There is an increasing array of legal websites on the Internet that may be worth trawling, but most provide quite minimalist levels of substantive advice and little or no advice on court or tribunal practice and procedure. Many of these sites simply signpost visitors on to more specialist sources of legal advice. An exception is the North Lambeth Law Centre's Racial Discrimination Unit website which includes a very useful do-it-yourself guide to the practice and procedure of racial discrimination cases in Employment Tribunals. The Unit also plans to provide training to litigants in person in due course.

LIST OF USEFUL ADDRESSES

Aire Centre
74 Eurolink Business Centre
49 Effra Road
London SW2 1BZ
Tel: 020 7924 0927
Fax: 020 7733 6786

Avon and Bristol Law Centre
2 Moon Street
Bristol BS2 8QE
Tel: 0117 924 8662
Fax: 0117 924 8020
Advice Line: 0117 924 8661

Bar Pro Bono Unit
7 Gray's Inn Square
Gray's Inn
London WC1R 5AZ
Tel: 020 7831 9711
Fax: 020 7831 9733

CITIZENS ADVICE BUREAU ADVICE GUIDE

Commission for Racial Equality
London
St Dunstan's House
201-211 Borough High Street
London SE1 1GZ
Tel: 020 7939 0000

Birmingham
Lancaster House
67 Newhall Street
Birmingham B3 1NA
Tel: 0121 710 3000

Leeds
Yorkshire Bank Chambers
Infirmary Street
Leeds LS1 2JP
Tel: 0113 389 3600

Manchester
Maybrook House
40 Blackfriars Street
Manchester M3 2EG
Tel: 0161 8355500

Scotland
Hanover House
45-51 Hanover Street
Edinburgh EH2 2PJ
Tel: 0131 226 5186

Wales
Capital Tower
Greyfriars Road
Cardiff CF1 3AG
Tel:029 2038 8977

Community Legal Service
To obtain one of the 13 CLS Regional Directories contact:

Resource Information Service
The Basement
38 Great Pulteney Street
London W1R 3DE
Tel: 020 7494 2408
Fax: 020 7287 8928

Discrimination Law Association
PO Box 20848
London SE22 0YP
Tel: 020 7450 3663
Fax: 020 7450 3664

Free Representation Unit
Fourth Floor
Peer House
8-14 Verulam Street
London WC1X 8LZ
Tel: 020 7831 0692

LAW CENTRES FEDERATION

London
Duchess House
18-19 Warren Street
London W1P 5DB
Tel: 020 738 78570

Manchester
3rd Floor
Elizabeth House
16 St Peters Square
Manchester M2 3DF
Tel: 0161 236 5333

The Law Society
113 Chancery Lane
London WC2A 1PL
Tel: 020 7242 1222

Liberty
21 Tabard Street
London SE1 4LA
Tel: 020 7403 3888
Fax: 020 7407 5354
Advice Line: 020 7378 8659
Monday and Thursday 6.00-8.00pm and Wednesday 12.30-2.30pm

Litigants in Person Society
Taunton
Somerset
Tel: 01823 324 002

National Convention of Black Teachers
PO Box 30
Pinner
Middlesex HA5 5HF

Northern Complainants Aid Fund
45 Westgate
Bradford
West Yorkshire
Tel: 01274 740 340

and

Midlands Unit
70 Villa Road
Handsworth
Birmingham B19 1BL
Tel: 0121 523 4411

North Lambeth Law Centre
The London Racial Discrimination Unit
14 Bowden Street
London SE11 4DS
Tel: 020 7793 0378

Public Law Project
Room E608
Birkbeck College
University of London
Malet Street
London WC1E 7HX
Tel: 020 7467 9800
Fax: 020 7467 9811
Public Law Advice Line: 020 7467 9807
Tuesdays and Thursdays 10am-1pm

Liberty and Public Law Project
Human Rights and Public Law Line 0808 808 4546
Monday and Wednesday 2.00pm – 5.00pm
Tuesday and Thursday 10.00am – 1.00pm
[NB For lawyers and advisers with a general civil contract from the Legal
Services Commission only]

Racial Equality Councils
Directory of names and addresses and websites for those which have them
can be found on the CRE's website. Details of individual RECs can be
obtained from CRE offices.

Trades Union Congress
Congress House
Great Russell Street
London WC1B 3LS
Tel: 020 7467 1294
Know Your Rights Telephone Line: 0870 6004 882

Beyond courtrooms: using the HRA in campaigning

Veena Vasista

Maximising the potential to challenge racism and racial discrimination involves much more than litigation. Proving discrimination will remain difficult and landmark cases challenging institutional racism will be rare. This is why it is important to use the HRA outside courtrooms and to integrate it into the day-to-day work of campaigning organisations.

Cultural shift

The Government has recognised that the HRA plays an important role in laying the foundation for a cultural shift in the UK. The Lord Chancellor said at the time of the Human Rights Bill that 'a culture of awareness of human rights will develop.' In the same debate, the Home Office Minister noted that 'every public authority will know that its behaviour, its structure, its conclusions and its executive actions will be subject to this culture.'

In this context, we should not view courts as the only place for principles of the HRA to be invoked. If your own organisation is concerned that legislation or policy violates the HRA, there is no need to wait for the moment when a case is being taken to court to draw attention to the human rights aspect of the issue. The HRA provides a framework for policy making and what could be considered a system of checks and balances for policy-makers. Therefore, while the courts might be the backdrop for challenges to policy-makers, ideally the process for guaranteeing human rights and freedoms will begin with highly informed (and principled) policy debates.

However, the HRA does not necessarily provide legislators and policy-makers with clear answers. For example, where it appears that rights are in conflict with each other (such as where unregulated freedom of speech extends to incitement to racial hatred), public authorities will have to measure their options carefully; and such sensitive decisions ought to be informed by the constituencies most affected by them. More frequently, policy-makers will be faced by claims that proposed policy violates the HRA. The balancing exercise in these instances will be not between different rights, but between government interests and the rights and freedoms of individuals. At times, within the parameters of the HRA, there may be legitimate justifications for such policy. Whatever the nature of the issue, what will be key in the policy debates around compliance is that decisions are made transparently and inclusively, guided by the human rights framework set out in the HRA.

In a broad cultural sense, however, the HRA also sends the message that society as a whole should embrace the principles underlying the law – equality, justice, dignity – and that individuals and public and private bodies should integrate them into their daily lives. To this end, for example, the newly developed citizenship education curriculum will have a human rights component to it. Thus, in the spirit of the HRA, *all* – and not just the Government of the day – will have a responsibility to respect the rights and dignity of others. The more that human rights concepts and principles are highlighted outside the courts, the greater is the chance that this wider cultural shift takes place.

To assist with this process, this chapter offers some suggestions for incorporating the HRA into day-to-day campaigning work to influence legislators and decision-makers.

Parliament
Ministers are expected to scrutinise new legislation for its compliance with the HRA. Before a Bill makes its way through parliament, the Minister concerned needs to prepare a Human Rights Impact Statement. This being the case, it is important that MPs receive views on its compliance, and correspondence to an MP offers the first campaigning opportunity. There is also a Joint Parliamentary Committee on Human Rights with the power to scrutinise legislation for human rights compliance. This Committee does not receive individual complaints, but correspondence can be sent to the Committee with reference to specific legislation and broad human rights concerns. The Committee is a key part of the parliamentary process for upholding human rights, and offers a second campaigning opportunity. It is important that any potential discriminatory impacts of legislation, within the parameters of Article 14 of the HRA, are brought to the attention of MPs, the Committee, and all legislators.

One should think broadly about this. This type of campaigning offers the scope to raise awareness of situations where it might be difficult in legal terms to prove an Article 14 violation, but there remains a legitimate concern regarding the impact of legislation on an individual's rights.

One example relates to the legal aid and legal services reforms. When these reforms were progressing through Parliament, many organisations claimed that they would impede access to the entire litigation process – and therefore access to justice – by people from certain communities. The point was that new legislation would be of little use if citizens did not have equal access to the courts to seek its protection.

Such campaigning does not require the threat of a particular court case, but broad debates on the principles at hand. Such debates draw attention to the more indirect ways in which human rights can be violated. Of course at the same time, with reference to the other sections of this book, one should be alert to the ways in which legislation might directly violate the rights of individuals from the specific communities with whom a lay organisation works.

Local government
Local authorities are, of course, public authorities for the purposes of the HRA. With a 'cultural shift', one would hope that human rights principles are eventually incorporated into the daily working life of local government. This process is similar to the way in which it is intended that equality principles are 'mainstreamed' into local government practices. Also, pressure should be put on local authorities to work in partnership with non-governmental organisations to promote the HRA and to put in place the necessary safeguards to prevent violations.

Many organisations find it useful to invite local authority representatives to speak to their members and their communities about what steps they are taking to implement and maintain respect for the HRA. If possible, such discussions should be with a range of departments. Organisations should speak to local policy makers about the issues raised throughout this book, such as school exclusions, stop and search, racial harassment, and the treatment of asylum seekers.

A constructive approach is for an organisation to make local government representatives aware that members of the communities with whom it works are fully aware of their rights, but also to emphasise that it is eager to help local government fulfill its responsibilities. And though the HRA primarily places responsibilities on public authorities, organisations should work with local government to educate people more generally about their rights, including their responsibility to respect the rights of all communities. It should be clear to government and the public alike that racism is a violation of human rights.

Media
It has always been an integral part of campaigning to use the media to promote human rights. This is explored in greater detail in the next chapter.

In short, where legitimate and relevant, organisations should make reference to potential human rights abuses when dealing with the media. Long before the HRA came into force, there was considerable rhetorical force in referring in vague terms to 'human rights abuses'. Ideally, however, there should now be reference to the HRA and, where possible, a specific Convention article.

Referring to the HRA can help also raise awareness of different interpretations of the rights protected under the HRA. This is important given that the HRA is supposed to be a 'living instrument' subject to re-interpretation. For example, if a racial equality adviser is talking to a journalist about a case of racial harassment in a housing estate, he or she should let the journalist know that racial harassment may be considered degrading and in violation of Article 3, and that the government has a responsibility to ensure equal protection of that right.

Human rights partnerships

Of course many organisations are small and lacking in resources. How can they find the time to analyse the human rights implications of a new piece of legislation or policy? This book will hopefully provide some pointers, but organisations should not be afraid of making use of established human rights groups. They should work in partnership with them.

For example, if draft legislation causing you concern is making its way through Parliament, contact Justice or Liberty and ask them if they are conducting a review of the legislation. Tell them your concerns, and ask it they might include them in their own submissions. Make the most of what such organisations have to offer.

Another useful approach, particularly for those outside London, might be to create a local or regional network of human rights experts: people you can contact regularly who might be more familiar with your local/regional situation and perhaps will be more available to speak, for example, at public meetings. These people might work for firms of solicitors, barristers' chambers, law centres or university law departments.

Human rights should not be segregated. There is no reason for ethnic minority organisations, individuals or communities to limit themselves to the racial equality dimensions of human rights. Organisations representing different racial, religious, and ethnic communities should also participate in human rights debates and discussions whether the topic is freedom of speech or the right to privacy. Part of the racial equality agenda is to ensure that policies in all areas of public life are informed by the range of communities affected by them (be it differently or in the same way).

International human rights standards generally

The HRA is based on the European Convention on Human Rights, which in turn was influenced by the Universal Declaration of Human Rights adopted by the United Nations in 1948. The UK has ratified a number of international human rights treaties and, while they cannot be enforced through the courts, they do place some obligations on the government.

Take, for example, the UN Convention for the Elimination of All Forms of Racial Discrimination. This treaty, ratified by the UK in 1969, obligates governments to 'condemn racial discrimination and undertake to pursue by all appropriate means and without delay a policy of eliminating racial discrimination in all its forms' (Article 2.1). It also specifically places an obligation on governments to carry out regular reviews of legislation and policy for their impact on racial equality and to amend where necessary. Organisations should refer to these obligations in their policy work and in representations to the media and local and national politicians. The UK government is itself regularly reviewed for its compliance with this and other treaties, and the UN publishes regular reports of its concerns and recommendations. These can be found on the United Nations website or obtained from organisations such as Liberty. Organisations should make reference to them.

There are a number of racial justice organisations in the UK that have been using international human rights mechanisms for many years, such as the Southall Black Sisters. Organisations working towards racial equality should connect with each other and learn from each other.

Racism as a violation of human rights

The idea of racism as a violation of human rights needs to become more than just a slogan. The international human rights community has carried out a lot of work on racism and racial discrimination, recently holding the UN World Conference Against Racism in South Africa (August 2001). The Conference produced a Declaration and Program of Action for challenging racism throughout the world (see the UN website for more information).

Perhaps not surprisingly, many of the action steps recommended are along the same lines as the underlying principles from the recommendations and conclusions of the inquiry into the murder of Stephen Lawrence. The Conference final documents show that challenging racism in a human rights framework boils down to multi-sector approaches: these include litigation, but also institutional reform, changes in policy-making processes, and public education.

In this context, saying that 'racism is a violation of human rights' means much more than saying it is a violation of law. Rather, it speaks to racism as undermining democratic values. It also serves as a reminder that when people claim they have been victims of racism or that the government must take more effective action to challenge racism, they are not asking for 'special' rights. They are asking for access to rights and freedoms belonging to everyone. Guaranteeing those rights is not a favour to anyone, but an obligation.

Using the media

Chris Myant

This chapter of the book deals with issues involved with handling the media. It could be subtitled: '... but use with care!'

Working with the media has to be part of any human rights toolkit. A free and campaigning media is a great ally in the work of those seeking to rid our society of abuses of human and civil rights. Uncovering injustice, exposing discrimination, pillorying those who perpetrate abuses are things that lie close the heart of any good journalist. Bringing together the media and human rights issues can be a powerful chemistry and, in exposing many injustices, the media has been a significant driving force in securing change.

In the digital and electronic age, the diversity of media outlets available to anyone seeking help in pinpointing injustice. Even those parts of the media that might be identified as critics of champions of human rights are often the very parts of the media which give considerable coverage to individual news stories on those themes, particularly where there is a strong human interest element available. This means that, whatever the issue, whatever the social sector involved, whatever the relevant audience you may want to reach, there is a publication, a radio programme, a website, and, with increasing likelihood, a television programme that will offer space.

Of course, coverage of these issues gains particular strength when it is seen to be driven by the independent judgment of the news media itself, rather than something offered at the say so of a self-interested lobby or campaigning group. But the fact remains that the media still sees the exposure of injustice as one of its primary functions, and so it will turn to those with the information and the contacts to provide it with such stories as well as probing for them independently.

However, this is just the start of the process. Before you pick up the telephone or dash off a press release, there are several tests to which you must subject every 'story'. You need to be sure before holding an individual's identity and personal experiences up to public view.

- What will be the consequences of publicity (and possibly denunciatory coverage) for the individual at the heart of the story?
- Will it rebound on those you are meant to be helping?
- They may well have won a justifiable and strong victory in a court of law, but is there something else in their life or activities that could come back to bite them?

Here are two true but salutary examples. One concerned an individual who had won a meritorious complaint of racial discrimination but who, in a separate incident at work some months earlier, had been caught with his fingers in the till for a petty amount of cash. The other concerned an oral announcement of a success in the Employment Tribunal that caught the complainant on the hop. Without anyone expecting it, a local news agency had a reporter and photographer on her home doorstep before the complainant had managed to get back home from the court. The photograph (which she did not realise had been taken from the other side of the street) then accompanied the splash story in the local daily the following morning. This she discovered only when she popped to her local newsagent to buy some chewing gum, to calm her nerves on her way to the first job interview she had managed to get since the dismissal which had led to the tribunal case!

An additional problem centres on a rather difficult question: is this a case where the media and the public can be expected to understand its relevance and meaning? The law as currently constituted can actually handle much litigation involving racial discrimination. One might well win a post-HRA case on the basis of a particularly arcane issue rather than an obviously wrong act. It can be difficult for journalists to present the case well or for the public to understand.

In racial discrimination cases, a further problem in recent years has been the size of the awards. For a start the media tends to centre on the money rather than the issue so, in a reported case, it is often hard for the public to grasp the nature of the hurt inflicted by the discrimination as justification for the seemingly vast sum. The more serious the damage inflicted, the greater the likelihood that the victim will be unwilling or unable to give media appearances; this may mean that even a favourable media may not be capable of getting the real flavour of the story across.

Another set of tests concern those championing the case or the cause. Do you really know what you are doing? Do you know the media? Do you have any real personal contacts? Who can you get advice from? These are almost technical issues. A media professional is driven by the needs of his or her job: a photograph, a quote or a bit of voice on tape must be obtained. An identifiable human being is needed, not a nameless cipher or statistic.

The media also tends to treat successful complaints in court cases in the same way that it treats anyone else passing through courts generally; which, unfortunately, means that journalists can approach a victim of discrimination in a similar way that they would a criminal. They assume they have a right to print their full home address for instance. In one case, a complainant who did not want her photograph printed in the paper was pictured in the *Daily Mail* running away from the court holding a paper bag to obscure her features with a posse of paparazzi chasing her down the street. Not the kind of dignity she had hoped to secure from her successful case.

There is much talk about using the power of the media to lever in further change or bring pressure to bear on defendants. On occasion it can be done with great and telling effect. However, a threat of adverse publicity which ends up as a couple of paragraphs on page 13 of the local paper looks rather like a case of the bark being worse than the bite. When those are the results of an attempt to generate adverse publicity, a client can feel completely deflated. It may also encourage the other side to think that they have got away with it.

Furthermore, you might easily achieve the coverage you want in the media *you* see (for example, a number of column inches in a national daily), but you may never be aware of the counter-attack by defendants in the specialist media you never see. A case in point in the autumn of 2000 was the coverage of the important success for the CRE in securing a County Court decision that Irish Travellers were within the meaning of a racial group as defined in the RRA. The case concerned the right of bar staff to refuse to serve such individuals. Coverage in the national press brought more complainants forward and enthused representative and advice groups. However, negative coverage in the trade press read by publicans was extensive and helped organise a counter push by certain publicans, who used the ploy of simply refusing service but giving no reason for doing so.

The overall message is simple: work hard. You have to work to secure good coverage, work hard to get the contacts in the media that really help, and work hard to make sure that the story is well based. You must also ensure that the individual at the centre of it is not vulnerable and that the message will get across: not just in the first headlines, but in a way that builds on the impact of the legal victory to secure wider and more lasting change.

There is another issue you must confront. What is your purpose when seeking media coverage of an issue or a case? Is the story intended to improve the profile of the work of an organisation, to satisfy a funder that its money has been well spent, or to make known the name of the campaign so that others may come forward with more cases? All these are laudable and even necessary aims, but putting a story around an individual's circumstances into a newspaper or onto a local radio news broadcast may not be the only way of fulfilling them. And, once in the public domain, any story can acquire a momentum of its own with consequences for the individuals concerned, not all of them positive.

When talking about day-to-day casework, we must also remember that the purpose of that work is to help the individual concerned, not to improve the reputation of the lawyers or the agency. Taking cases can be very gruelling for an individual. Extensive media coverage, intrusion into a person's private life or, on some occasions, giving a public profile to an individual who needs privacy, can all be devastating. Most agencies working in the discrimination, human rights and related fields are good at handling the case up to the point of victory, but tend to do very little by way of 'after-case care'. The individuals usually just disappear back into the woodwork, carrying their pain and sometimes their dissatisfaction with them.

It stands to reason that a complainant destroyed in the media through adverse coverage will discourage other individuals with grievances from coming forward, so much so that the negative effect of poor media treatment can often outweigh the positive value of a number of other good stories. To those who have put their heads about the parapet, and those have been hurt further as a consequence, and those who have yet to take the plunge, we have a responsibility to make sure that we not only the law right, but that we also make the media work right.

The consequences of failing to do so can be horrific. One case I was involved in related to a person who won a good and solidly grounded racial discrimination case in the Employment Tribunal, but who had the case consistently misrepresented in the national media. There was a splash in the *Daily Mail*, followed by a feature double page spread in the same paper. It gave a full-face photograph of him and an indication of his partner's place of work. He had to have his letters redirected via the local police station because of the volume of hate mail, he had photographers camped outside his home for days, he and his child had to make the school journey over the back fence each day and his partner was harassed at work by journalists. For several weeks, he had rubbish skips delivered to his home address as a result of malevolent orders put by someone over the telephone. The problem for me was that, while I could see the clear injustice that he had suffered, the media could not.

It was not the *Mail* itself that set the hare running, but a local daily that did so on the basis of a false story line about the complainant leaked to the paper by the employer. Unusually, through an accident of the way in which the smear was leaked, we were able to prove that it came from the employer. Subsequently, we were able to impose an agreement in which the employer agreed to absolute silence.

In another recent case in which I was involved, an Employment Tribunal recorded a success for a black rugby player who alleged racial discrimination after being dropped from his team. The story was given some coverage in the local media and the *Guardian* followed up with a supportively worded feature that I helped to arrange. Subsequently, the *Independent* carried a feature discussing the case that contained several criticisms of the complainant, implying that he was a 'money-grabber' and that he had merely been an ageing player who did not know when to quit. The piece in the *Independent* raised some very interesting and legitimate points around the case, but it left a strong feeling in the reader's mind that the basis of the case may have been phoney. Did the totality of the coverage add or subtract from the cause of the individual at the centre?

The point is this. Although we sometimes choose parts of the media with a reputation for understanding the issues, those with a different interpretation have every right to pick up the story and run with it in whatever way they choose. The delivery of justice is a public process, and others have an equal right and capacity to subject the story to debate. Regulatory bodes in the media may eventually be of help, but only long after the damage has been inflicted. The Press Complaints Commission covering the newspaper is perhaps the least helpful of all. And, if the PCC turns the complaint down, the damage is amplified.

The traffic of cases to the media is no longer a one-way street. Defendants in cases are fully able to put their own point of view and to do so without ever having to go on the public record. Just as we now have solicitors advertising their litigation services on cinema screens, so we also have skilled professionals providing their expertise to those who wish to counter the impact of successful court cases exposing abuses. Some of the training on offer to employers and others in the wake of the HRA has been less about eradicating malpractice than how to 'duck and dive' through the courts or counter-attack in the media.

Discouraged? Don't be. You would go into the legal side of a complaint determined to know the strengths of the other side's case, and must do exactly the same when it comes to using the media. As professionals, we have no right to use the lives of the vulnerable as cannonballs in *our* struggle. We have a media that is increasingly equipped to give coverage to these kind of issues.

Summary

So, try to ensure that you:

- **Think about media coverage as a case develops**
  Discuss the pros and cons with the client. Make sure that he or she is comfortable with the potential publicity, knows what to say and how to say it, has the confidence to say it effectively, has no skeletons in the cupboard, and no difficulties into which he or she may later run.
- **Develop your contacts with the media**
  Listen to and read the media. There are big differences out there. Local radio is different to national television news or the press. The new websites are eager for news, but they are often produced by relatively unskilled operators and often have few readers. What might make a small story in a local newspaper could build into a significant feature on the BBC local radio or make a useful human interest story for a subsequent television documentary. Whatever the medium you are thinking of, there is no point in *approaching* it if you do not *know* it. Build personal contacts in the most simple and direct way, by just telephoning and asking to see people. If you need advice and help in any of this, many of us working in this field would be happy to offer advice and contacts.
- **Look at other ways for using the material your case work generates**
  If you handle more than one case, reports with anonymous examples can have a greater impact. If you have a regular workload, get the media to help you. Journalists can uncover much evidence if they know what they are looking for and are able to use modern media techniques.
- **Follow through with clients**
  Don't lose touch with those who have won cases. Media coverage in documentaries, or referring to a case subsequently, to illustrate points when related national reports appear, can be more extensive and more effective in getting the message across. It can also be easier for the individual themselves to deliver as the immediate tension of the case has died away and, hopefully, his or her life is back on track. Litigation can be gruelling and people may need solidarity and support long after the court doors have closed behind them.
- **Don't be afraid of the media, but know its dangers**
  Without investigative journalism and good news coverage, we will never secure human rights, but there is no free ticket to success. Look and see if the case and those at its centre can carry coverage, get the technical arrangements right, make sure the individual knows what is at stake and can handle it, and don't be afraid to decide *against* media coverage if that seems the more sensible thing to do.

APPENDIX

Below is a transcript of key parts of the Human Rights Act 1998. Parts of the HRA beyond the scope of this book have been omitted.

HUMAN RIGHTS ACT 1998

An Act to give further effect to rights and freedoms guaranteed under the European Convention on Human Rights; to make provision with respect to holders of certain judicial offices who become judges of the European Court of Human Rights; and for connected purposes.

[9th November 1998]

BE IT ENACTED by the Queen's most Excellent Majesty, by and with the advice and consent of the Lords Spiritual and Temporal, and Commons, in this present Parliament assembled, and by the authority of the same, as follows:

INTRODUCTION

The Convention Rights

1. – (1) In this Act 'the Convention rights' means the rights and fundamental freedoms set out in –
    (a) Articles 2 to 12 and 14 of the Convention,
    (b) Articles 1 to 3 of the First Protocol, and
    (c) Articles 1 and 2 of the Sixth Protocol, as read with Articles 16 to 18 of the Convention.

    (2) Those Articles are to have effect for the purposes of this Act subject to any designated derogation or reservation (as to which see sections 14 and 15).

(3) The Articles are set out in Schedule 1.

(4) The Secretary of State may by order make such amendments to this Act as he considers appropriate to reflect the effect, in relation to the United Kingdom, of a protocol.

(5) In subsection (4) 'protocol' means a protocol to the Convention –
  (a) which the United Kingdom has ratified; or
  (b) which the United Kingdom has signed with a view to ratification.

(6) No amendment may be made by an order under subsection (4) so as to come into force before the protocol concerned is in force in relation to the United Kingdom.

Interpretation of Convention rights

2. – (1) A court or tribunal determining a question which has arisen in connection with a Convention right must take into account any –
  (a) judgment, decision, declaration or advisory opinion of the European Court of Human Rights,
  (b) opinion of the Commission given in a report adopted under Article 31 of the Convention,
  (c) decision of the Commission in connection with Article 26 or 27(2) of the Convention, or
  (d) decision of the Committee of Ministers taken under Article 46 of the Convention, whenever made or given, so far as, in the opinion of the court or tribunal, it is relevant to the proceedings in which that question has arisen.

(2) Evidence of any judgment, decision, declaration or opinion of which account may have to be taken under this section is to be given in proceedings before any court or tribunal in such manner as may be provided by rules.

(3) In this section 'rules' means rules of court or, in the case of proceedings before a tribunal, rules made for the purposes of this section –
  (a) by the Lord Chancellor or the Secretary of State, in relation to any proceedings outside Scotland;
  (b) by the Secretary of State, in relation to proceedings in Scotland; or
  (c) by a Northern Ireland department, in relation to proceedings before a tribunal in Northern Ireland –
  (i) which deals with transferred matters; and
  (ii) for which no rules made under paragraph (a) are in force.

LEGISLATION

Interpretation of legislation

3. – (1) So far as it is possible to do so, primary legislation and subordinate legislation must be read and given effect in a way which is compatible with the Convention rights.

(2) This section –
   (a) applies to primary legislation and subordinate legislation whenever enacted;
   (b) does not affect the validity, continuing operation or enforcement of any incompatible primary legislation; and
   (c) does not affect the validity, continuing operation or enforcement of any incompatible subordinate legislation if (disregarding any possibility of revocation) primary legislation prevents removal of the incompatibility.

Declaration of incompatibility

4. – (1) Subsection (2) applies in any proceedings in which a court determines whether a provision of primary legislation is compatible with a Convention right.

(2) If the court is satisfied that the provision is incompatible with a Convention right, it may make a declaration of that incompatibility.

(3) Subsection (4) applies in any proceedings in which a court determines whether a provision of subordinate legislation, made in the exercise of a power conferred by primary legislation, is compatible with a Convention right.

(4) If the court is satisfied –
   (a) that the provision is incompatible with a Convention right, and
   (b) that (disregarding any possibility of revocation) the primary legislation concerned prevents removal of the incompatibility, it may make a declaration of that incompatibility.

(5) In this section 'court' means –
   (a) the House of Lords;
   (b) the Judicial Committee of the Privy Council;
   (c) the Courts-Martial Appeal Court;
   (d) in Scotland, the High Court of Justiciary sitting otherwise than as a trial court or the Court of Session;
   (e) in England and Wales or Northern Ireland, the High Court or the Court of Appeal.

(6) A declaration under this section ('a declaration of incompatibility') –
   (a) does not affect the validity, continuing operation or enforcement of the provision in respect of which it is given; and
   (b) is not binding on the parties to the proceedings in which it is made.

Right of Crown to intervene

5. – (1) Where a court is considering whether to make a declaration of incompatibility, the Crown is entitled to notice in accordance with rules of court.

(2) In any case to which subsection (1) applies –
   (a) a Minister of the Crown (or a person nominated by him),
   (b) a member of the Scottish Executive,
   (c) a Northern Ireland Minister,
   (d) a Northern Ireland department, is entitled, on giving notice in accordance with rules of court, to be joined as a party to the proceedings.

(3) Notice under subsection (2) may be given at any time during the proceedings.

(4) A person who has been made a party to criminal proceedings (other than in Scotland) as the result of a notice under subsection (2) may, with leave, appeal to the House of Lords against any declaration of incompatibility made in the proceedings.

(5) In subsection (4) –
   'criminal proceedings' includes all proceedings before the Courts-Martial Appeal Court; and 'leave' means leave granted by the court making the declaration of incompatibility or by the House of Lords.

PUBLIC AUTHORITIES

Acts of public authorities

6. – (1) It is unlawful for a public authority to act in a way which is incompatible with a Convention right.

(2) Subsection (1) does not apply to an act if –
   (a) as the result of one or more provisions of primary legislation, the authority could not have acted differently; or
   (b) in the case of one or more provisions of, or made under, primary legislation which cannot be read or given effect in a way which

is compatible with the Convention rights, the authority was acting so as to give effect to or enforce those provisions.

(3) In this section 'public authority' includes –
  (a) a court or tribunal, and
  (b) any person certain of whose functions are functions of a public nature, but does not include either House of Parliament or a person exercising functions in connection with proceedings in Parliament.

(4) In subsection (3) 'Parliament' does not include the House of Lords in its judicial capacity.

(5) In relation to a particular act, a person is not a public authority by virtue only of subsection (3)(b) if the nature of the act is private.

(6) 'An act' includes a failure to act but does not include a failure to –
  (a) introduce in, or lay before, Parliament a proposal for legislation; or
  (b) make any primary legislation or remedial order.

Proceedings

7. – (1) A person who claims that a public authority has acted (or proposes to act) in a way which is made unlawful by section 6(1) may –
  (a) bring proceedings against the authority under this Act in the appropriate court or tribunal, or
  (b) rely on the Convention right or rights concerned in any legal proceedings, but only if he is (or would be) a victim of the unlawful act.

(2) In subsection (1)(a) 'appropriate court or tribunal' means such court or tribunal as may be determined in accordance with rules; and proceedings against an authority include a counterclaim or similar proceeding.

(3) If the proceedings are brought on an application for judicial review, the applicant is to be taken to have a sufficient interest in relation to the unlawful act only if he is, or would be, a victim of that act.

(4) If the proceedings are made by way of a petition for judicial review in Scotland, the applicant shall be taken to have title and interest to sue in relation to the unlawful act only if he is, or would be, a victim of that act.

(5) Proceedings under subsection (1)(a) must be brought before the end of –
  (a) the period of one year beginning with the date on which the act complained of took place; or

(b) such longer period as the court or tribunal considers equitable having regard to all the circumstances, but that is subject to any rule imposing a stricter time limit in relation to the procedure in question.

(6) In subsection (1)(b) 'legal proceedings' includes –
(a) proceedings brought by or at the instigation of a public authority; and
(b) an appeal against the decision of a court or tribunal.

(7) For the purposes of this section, a person is a victim of an unlawful act only if he would be a victim for the purposes of Article 34 of the Convention if proceedings were brought in the European Court of Human Rights in respect of that act.

(8) Nothing in this Act creates a criminal offence.

(9) In this section 'rules' means –
(a) in relation to proceedings before a court or tribunal outside Scotland, rules made by the Lord Chancellor or the Secretary of State for the purposes of this section or rules of court,
(b) in relation to proceedings before a court or tribunal in Scotland, rules made by the Secretary of State for those purposes,
(c) in relation to proceedings before a tribunal in Northern Ireland –
(i) which deals with transferred matters, and
(ii) for which no rules made under paragraph (a) are in force, rules made by a Northern Ireland department for those purposes, and includes provision made by order under section 1 of the Courts and Legal Services Act 1990.

(10) In making rules, regard must be had to section 9.

(11) The Minister who has power to make rules in relation to a particular tribunal may, to the extent he considers it necessary to ensure that the tribunal can provide an appropriate remedy in relation to an act (or proposed act) of a public authority which is (or would be) unlawful as a result of section 6(1), by order add to –
(a) the relief or remedies which the tribunal may grant; or
(b) the grounds on which it may grant any of them.

(12) An order made under subsection (11) may contain such incidental, supplemental, consequential or transitional provision as the Minister making it considers appropriate.

(13)'The Minister' includes the Northern Ireland department concerned.

Judicial remedies

8. – (1) In relation to any act (or proposed act) of a public authority which the court finds is (or would be) unlawful, it may grant such relief or remedy, or make such order, within its powers as it considers just and appropriate.

(2) But damages may be awarded only by a court which has power to award damages, or to order the payment of compensation, in civil proceedings.

(3) No award of damages is to be made unless, taking account of all the circumstances of the case, including –

  (a) any other relief or remedy granted, or order made, in relation to the act in question (by that or any other court), and

  (b) the consequences of any decision (of that or any other court) in respect of that act, the court is satisfied that the award is necessary to afford just satisfaction to the person in whose favour it is made.

(4) In determining –

  (a) whether to award damages, or

  (b) the amount of an award, the court must take into account the principles applied by the European Court of Human Rights in relation to the award of compensation under Article 41 of the Convention.

(5) A public authority against which damages are awarded is to be treated –

  (a) in Scotland, for the purposes of section 3 of the Law Reform (Miscellaneous Provisions) (Scotland) Act 1940 as if the award were made in an action of damages in which the authority has been found liable in respect of loss or damage to the person to whom the award is made;

  (b) for the purposes of the Civil Liability (Contribution) Act 1978 as liable in respect of damage suffered by the person to whom the award is made.

(6) In this section –

  'court' includes a tribunal;

  'damages' means damages for an unlawful act of a public authority; and

  'unlawful' means unlawful under section 6(1).

Judicial acts

9. – (1) Proceedings under section 7(1)(a) in respect of a judicial act may be brought only –

   (a) by exercising a right of appeal;

   (b) on an application (in Scotland a petition) for judicial review; or

   (c) in such other forum as may be prescribed by rules.

(2) That does not affect any rule of law which prevents a court from being the subject of judicial review.

(3) In proceedings under this Act in respect of a judicial act done in good faith, damages may not be awarded otherwise than to compensate a person to the extent required by Article 5(5) of the Convention.

(4) An award of damages permitted by subsection (3) is to be made against the Crown; but no award may be made unless the appropriate person, if not a party to the proceedings, is joined.

(5) In this section –

'appropriate person' means the Minister responsible for the court concerned, or a person or government department nominated by him;

'court' includes a tribunal;

'judge' includes a member of a tribunal, a justice of the peace and a clerk or other officer entitled to exercise the jurisdiction of a court;

'judicial act' means a judicial act of a court and includes an act done on the instructions, or on behalf, of a judge; and

'rules' has the same meaning as in section 7(9).

REMEDIAL ACTION

Power to take remedial action

10. – (1) This section applies if –

   (a) a provision of legislation has been declared under section 4 to be incompatible with a Convention right and, if an appeal lies –

   (i) all persons who may appeal have stated in writing that they do not intend to do so;

   (ii) the time for bringing an appeal has expired and no appeal has been brought within that time; or

   (iii) an appeal brought within that time has been determined or abandoned; or

(b) it appears to a Minister of the Crown or Her Majesty in Council that, having regard to a finding of the European Court of Human Rights made after the coming into force of this section in proceedings against the United Kingdom, a provision of legislation is incompatible with an obligation of the United Kingdom arising from the Convention.

(2) If a Minister of the Crown considers that there are compelling reasons for proceeding under this section, he may by order make such amendments to the legislation as he considers necessary to remove the incompatibility.

(3) If, in the case of subordinate legislation, a Minister of the Crown considers –

(a) that it is necessary to amend the primary legislation under which the subordinate legislation in question was made, in order to enable the incompatibility to be removed, and

(b) that there are compelling reasons for proceeding under this section, he may by order make such amendments to the primary legislation as he considers necessary.

(4) This section also applies where the provision in question is in subordinate legislation and has been quashed, or declared invalid, by reason of incompatibility with a Convention right and the Minister proposes to proceed under paragraph 2(b) of Schedule 2.

(5) If the legislation is an Order in Council, the power conferred by subsection (2) or (3) is exercisable by Her Majesty in Council.

(6) In this section 'legislation' does not include a Measure of the Church Assembly or of the General Synod of the Church of England.

(7) Schedule 2 makes further provision about remedial orders.

OTHER RIGHTS AND PROCEEDINGS

Safeguard for existing human rights

11. – A person's reliance on a Convention right does not restrict –

(a) any other right or freedom conferred on him by or under any law having effect in any part of the United Kingdom; or

(b) his right to make any claim or bring any proceedings which he could make or bring apart from sections 7 to 9.

Freedom of expression

12. – (1) This section applies if a court is considering whether to grant any relief which, if granted, might affect the exercise of the Convention right to freedom of expression.

(2) If the person against whom the application for relief is made ('the respondent') is neither present nor represented, no such relief is to be granted unless the court is satisfied –
  (a) that the applicant has taken all practicable steps to notify the respondent; or
  (b) that there are compelling reasons why the respondent should not be notified.

(3) No such relief is to be granted so as to restrain publication before trial unless the court is satisfied that the applicant is likely to establish that publication should not be allowed.

(4) The court must have particular regard to the importance of the Convention right to freedom of expression and, where the proceedings relate to material which the respondent claims, or which appears to the court, to be journalistic, literary or artistic material (or to conduct connected with such material), to –
  (a) the extent to which –
    (i) the material has, or is about to, become available to the public, or
    (ii) it is, or would be, in the public interest for the material to be published;
  (b) any relevant privacy code.

(5) In this section –
  'court' includes a tribunal; and
  'relief' includes any remedy or order (other than in criminal proceedings).

Freedom of thought, conscience and religion

13. – (1) If a court's determination of any question arising under this Act might affect the exercise by a religious organisation (itself or its members collectively) of the Convention right to freedom of thought, conscience and religion, it must have particular regard to the importance of that right.

(2) In this section 'court' includes a tribunal.

PARLIAMENTARY PROCEDURE

Statements of compatibility

19. – (1) A Minister of the Crown in charge of a Bill in either House of Parliament must, before Second Reading of the Bill –

   (a) make a statement to the effect that in his view the provisions of the Bill are compatible with the Convention rights ('a statement of compatibility'); or

   (b) make a statement to the effect that although he is unable to make a statement of compatibility the government nevertheless wishes the House to proceed with the Bill.

(2) The statement must be in writing and be published in such manner as the Minister making it considers appropriate.

SUPPLEMENTAL

Orders etc under this Act

20. – (1) Any power of a Minister of the Crown to make an order under this Act is exercisable by statutory instrument.

(2) The power of the Lord Chancellor or the Secretary of State to make rules (other than rules of court) under section 2(3) or 7(9) is exercisable by statutory instrument.

(3) Any statutory instrument made under section 14, 15 or 16(7) must be laid before Parliament.

(4) No order may be made by the Lord Chancellor or the Secretary of State under section 1(4), 7(11) or 16(2) unless a draft of the order has been laid before, and approved by, each House of Parliament.

(5) Any statutory instrument made under section 18(7) or Schedule 4, or to which subsection (2) applies, shall be subject to annulment in pursuance of a resolution of either House of Parliament.

(6) The power of a Northern Ireland department to make –

   (a) rules under section 2(3)(c) or 7(9)(c), or

   (b) an order under section 7(11), is exercisable by statutory rule for the purposes of the Statutory Rules (Northern Ireland) Order 1979.

(7) Any rules made under section 2(3)(c) or 7(9)(c) shall be subject to

negative resolution; and section 41(6) of the Interpretation Act Northern Ireland) 1954 (meaning of 'subject to negative resolution') shall apply as if the power to make the rules were conferred by an Act of the Northern Ireland Assembly.

(8) No order may be made by a Northern Ireland department under section 7(11) unless a draft of the order has been laid before, and approved by, the Northern Ireland Assembly.

Interpretation, etc

21. – (1) In this Act –

'amend' includes repeal and apply (with or without modifications);

'the appropriate Minister' means the Minister of the Crown having charge of the appropriate authorised government department (within the meaning of the Crown Proceedings Act 1947);

'the Commission' means the European Commission of Human Rights;

'the Convention' means the Convention for the Protection of Human Rights and Fundamental Freedoms, agreed by the Council of Europe at Rome on 4th November 1950 as it has effect for the time being in relation to the United Kingdom;

'declaration of incompatibility' means a declaration under section 4;

'Minister of the Crown' has the same meaning as in the Ministers of the Crown Act 1975;

'Northern Ireland Minister' includes the First Minister and the deputy First Minister in Northern Ireland;

'primary legislation' means any –

(a) public general Act;

(b) local and personal Act;

(c) private Act;

(d) Measure of the Church Assembly;

(e) Measure of the General Synod of the Church of England;

(f) Order in Council –

(i) made in exercise of Her Majesty's Royal Prerogative;

(ii) made under section 38(1)(a) of the Northern Ireland Constitution Act 1973 or the corresponding provision of the Northern Ireland Act 1998; or

(iii) amending an Act of a kind mentioned in paragraph (a), (b) or (c);

and includes an order or other instrument made under primary legislation (otherwise than by the National Assembly for Wales, a member of the Scottish Executive, a Northern Ireland Minister or a Northern Ireland department) to the extent to which it operates to bring one or more provisions of that legislation into force or amends any primary legislation;

'the First Protocol' means the protocol to the Convention agreed at Paris on 20th March 1952;

'the Sixth Protocol' means the protocol to the Convention agreed at Strasbourg on 28th April 1983;

'the Eleventh Protocol' means the protocol to the Convention (restructuring the control machinery established by the Convention) agreed at Strasbourg on 11th May 1994;

'remedial order' means an order under section 10;

'subordinate legislation' means any –

(a)　Order in Council other than one –

(i) made in exercise of Her Majesty's Royal Prerogative;

(ii) made under section 38(1)(a) of the Northern Ireland Constitution Act 1973 or the corresponding provision of the Northern Ireland Act 1998; or

(iii) amending an Act of a kind mentioned in the definition of primary legislation;

(b)　Act of the Scottish Parliament;

(c)　Act of the Parliament of Northern Ireland;

(d)　Measure of the Assembly established under section 1 of the Northern Ireland Assembly Act 1973;

(e)　Act of the Northern Ireland Assembly;

(f)　order, rules, regulations, scheme, warrant, byelaw or other instrument made under primary legislation (except to the extent to which it operates to bring one or more provisions of that legislation into force or amends any primary legislation);

(g)　order, rules, regulations, scheme, warrant, byelaw or other instrument made under legislation mentioned in paragraph (b), (c), (d) or (e) or made under an Order in Council applying only to Northern Ireland;

(h)　order, rules, regulations, scheme, warrant, byelaw or other instrument made by a member of the Scottish Executive, a Northern Ireland Minister or a Northern Ireland department in exercise of prerogative or other executive functions of Her Majesty which are exercisable by such a person on behalf of Her Majesty;

'transferred matters' has the same meaning as in the Northern Ireland Act 1998; and 'tribunal' means any tribunal in which legal proceedings may be brought.

(2) The references in paragraphs (b) and (c) of section 2(1) to Articles are to Articles of the Convention as they had effect immediately before the coming into force of the Eleventh Protocol.

(3) The reference in paragraph (d) of section 2(1) to Article 46 includes a reference to Articles 32 and 54 of the Convention as they had effect immediately before the coming into force of the Eleventh Protocol.

(4) The references in section 2(1) to a report or decision of the Commission or a decision of the Committee of Ministers include references to a report or decision made as provided by paragraphs 3, 4 and 6 of Article 5 of the Eleventh Protocol (transitional provisions).

(5) Any liability under the Army Act 1955, the Air Force Act 1955 or the Naval Discipline Act 1957 to suffer death for an offence is replaced by a liability to imprisonment for life or any less punishment authorised by those Acts; and those Acts shall accordingly have effect with the necessary modifications.

Short title, commencement, application and extent

22. – (1) This Act may be cited as the Human Rights Act 1998.

(2) Sections 18, 20 and 21(5) and this section come into force on the passing of this Act.

(3) The other provisions of this Act come into force on such day as the Secretary of State may by order appoint; and different days may be appointed for different purposes.

(4) Paragraph (b) of subsection (1) of section 7 applies to proceedings brought by or at the instigation of a public authority whenever the act in question took place; but otherwise that subsection does not apply to an act taking place before the coming into force of that section.

(5) This Act binds the Crown.

(6) This Act extends to Northern Ireland.

(7) Section 21(5), so far as it relates to any provision contained in the Army Act 1955, the Air Force Act 1955 or the Naval Discipline Act 1957, extends to any place to which that provision extends.

SCHEDULES

Schedule 1

THE ARTICLES

PART I: THE CONVENTION

Rights and Freedoms

Article 2

Right to Life

1. Everyone's right to life shall be protected by law. No one shall be deprived of his life intentionally save in the execution of a sentence of a court following his conviction of a crime for which this penalty is provided by law.

2. Deprivation of life shall not be regarded as inflicted in contravention of this Article when it results from the use of force which is no more than absolutely necessary:
   (a) in defence of any person from unlawful violence;
   (b) in order to effect a lawful arrest or to prevent the escape of a person lawfully detained;
   (c) in action lawfully taken for the purpose of quelling a riot or insur-rection.

Article 3

Prohibition of Torture

No one shall be subjected to torture or to inhuman or degrading treatment or punishment.

Article 4

Prohibition of Slavery and Forced Labour

1. No one shall be held in slavery or servitude.

2. No one shall be required to perform forced or compulsory labour.

3. For the purpose of this Article the term 'forced or compulsory labour' shall not include:

(a) any work required to be done in the ordinary course of detention imposed according to the provisions of Article 5 of this Convention or during conditional release from such detention;
(b) any service of a military character or, in case of conscientious objectors in countries where they are recognised, service exacted instead of compulsory military service;
(c) any service exacted in case of an emergency or calamity threatening the life or well-being of the community;
(d) any work or service which forms part of normal civic obligations.

Article 5

Right to Liberty and Security

1. Everyone has the right to liberty and security of person. No one shall be deprived of his liberty save in the following cases and in accordance with a procedure prescribed by law:
   (a) the lawful detention of a person after conviction by a competent court;
   (b) the lawful arrest or detention of a person for non-compliance with the lawful order of a court or in order to secure the fulfilment of any obligation prescribed by law;
   (c) the lawful arrest or detention of a person effected for the purpose of bringing him before the competent legal authority on reasonable suspicion of having committed an offence or when it is reasonably considered necessary to prevent his committing an offence or fleeing after having done so;
   (d) the detention of a minor by lawful order for the purpose of educational supervision or his lawful detention for the purpose of bringing him before the competent legal authority;
   (e) the lawful detention of persons for the prevention of the spreading of infectious diseases, of persons of unsound mind, alcoholics or drug addicts or vagrants;
   (f) the lawful arrest or detention of a person to prevent his effecting an unauthorised entry into the country or of a person against whom action is being taken with a view to deportation or extradition.

2. Everyone who is arrested shall be informed promptly, in a language which he understands, of the reasons for his arrest and of any charge against him.

3. Everyone arrested or detained in accordance with the provisions of paragraph 1(c) of this Article shall be brought promptly before a judge or other officer authorised by law to exercise judicial power and shall be entitled to

trial within a reasonable time or to release pending trial. Release may be conditioned by guarantees to appear for trial.

4. Everyone who is deprived of his liberty by arrest or detention shall be entitled to take proceedings by which the lawfulness of his detention shall be decided speedily by a court and his release ordered if the detention is not lawful.

5. Everyone who has been the victim of arrest or detention in contravention of the provisions of this Article shall have an enforceable right to compensation.

Article 6

Right to a Fair Trial

1. In the determination of his civil rights and obligations or of any criminal charge against him, everyone is entitled to a fair and public hearing within a reasonable time by an independent and impartial tribunal established by law. Judgment shall be pronounced publicly but the press and public may be excluded from all or part of the trial in the interest of morals, public order or national security in a democratic society, where the interests of juveniles or the protection of the private life of the parties so require, or to the extent strictly necessary in the opinion of the court in special circumstances where publicity would prejudice the interests of justice.

2. Everyone charged with a criminal offence shall be presumed innocent until proved guilty according to law.

3. Everyone charged with a criminal offence has the following minimum rights:
   (a) to be informed promptly, in a language which he understands and in detail, of the nature and cause of the accusation against him;
   (b) to have adequate time and facilities for the preparation of his defence;
   (c) to defend himself in person or through legal assistance of his own choosing or, if he has not sufficient means to pay for legal assistance, to be given it free when the interests of justice so require;
   (d) to examine or have examined witnesses against him and to obtain the attendance and examination of witnesses on his behalf under the same conditions as witnesses against him;
   (e) to have the free assistance of an interpreter if he cannot understand or speak the language used in court.

Article 7

No Punishment Without Law

1. No one shall be held guilty of any criminal offence on account of any act or omission which did not constitute a criminal offence under national or international law at the time when it was committed. Nor shall a heavier penalty be imposed than the one that was applicable at the time the criminal offence was committed.

2. This Article shall not prejudice the trial and punishment of any person for any act or omission which, at the time when it was committed, was criminal according to the general principles of law recognised by civilised nations.

Article 8

Right to Respect for Private and Family Life

1. Everyone has the right to respect for his private and family life, his home and his correspondence.

2. There shall be no interference by a public authority with the exercise of this right except such as is in accordance with the law and is necessary in a democratic society in the interests of national security, public safety or the economic well-being of the country, for the prevention of disorder or crime, for the protection of health or morals, or for the protection of the rights and freedoms of others.

Article 9

Freedom of Thought, Conscience and Religion

1. Everyone has the right to freedom of thought, conscience and religion; this right includes freedom to change his religion or belief and freedom, either alone or in community with others and in public or private, to manifest his religion or belief, in worship, teaching, practice and observance.

2. Freedom to manifest one's religion or beliefs shall be subject only to such limitations as are prescribed by law and are necessary in a democratic society in the interests of public safety, for the protection of public order, health or morals, or for the protection of the rights and freedoms of others.

Article 10

Freedom of Expression

1. Everyone has the right to freedom of expression. This right shall include

freedom to hold opinions and to receive and impart information and ideas without interference by public authority and regardless of frontiers. This Article shall not prevent States from requiring the licensing of broadcasting, television or cinema enterprises.

2. The exercise of these freedoms, since it carries with it duties and responsibilities, may be subject to such formalities, conditions, restrictions or penalties as are prescribed by law and are necessary in a democratic society, in the interests of national security, territorial integrity or public safety, for the prevention of disorder or crime, for the protection of health or morals, for the protection of the reputation or rights of others, for preventing the disclosure of information received in confidence, or for maintaining the authority and impartiality of the judiciary.

Article 11

Freedom of Assembly and Association

1. Everyone has the right to freedom of peaceful assembly and to freedom of association with others, including the right to form and to join trade unions for the protection of his interests.

2. No restrictions shall be placed on the exercise of these rights other than such as are prescribed by law and are necessary in a democratic society in the interests of national security or public safety, for the prevention of disorder or crime, for the protection of health or morals or for the protection of the rights and freedoms of others. This Article shall not prevent the imposition of lawful restrictions on the exercise of these rights by members of the armed forces, of the police or of the administration of the State.

Article 12

Right to Marry

Men and women of marriageable age have the right to marry and to found a family, according to the national laws governing the exercise of this right.

Article 14

Prohibition of Discrimination

The enjoyment of the rights and freedoms set forth in this Convention shall be secured without discrimination on any ground such as sex, race, colour, language, religion, political or other opinion, national or social origin, association with a national minority, property, birth or other status.

Article 16

Restrictions on Political Activity of Aliens

Nothing in Articles 10, 11 and 14 shall be regarded as preventing the High Contracting Parties from imposing restrictions on the political activity of aliens.

Article 17

Prohibition of Abuse of Rights

Nothing in this Convention may be interpreted as implying for any State, group or person any right to engage in any activity or perform any act aimed at the destruction of any of the rights and freedoms set forth herein or at their limitation to a greater extent than is provided for in the Convention.

Article 18

Limitation on Use of Restrictions on Rights

The restrictions permitted under this Convention to the said rights and freedoms shall not be applied for any purpose other than those for which they have been prescribed.

PART II: THE FIRST PROTOCOL

Article 1

Protection of Property

Every natural or legal person is entitled to the peaceful enjoyment of his possessions. No one shall be deprived of his possessions except in the public interest and subject to the conditions provided for by law and by the general principles of international law.

The preceding provisions shall not, however, in any way impair the right of a State to enforce such laws as it deems necessary to control the use of property in accordance with the general interest or to secure the payment of taxes or other contributions or penalties.

Article 2

Right to Education

No person shall be denied the right to education. In the exercise of any functions which it assumes in relation to education and to teaching, the State shall respect the right of parents to ensure such education and teaching in conformity with their own religious and philosophical convictions.

Article 3

Right to Free Elections
The High Contracting Parties undertake to hold free elections at reasonable intervals by secret ballot, under conditions which will ensure the free expression of the opinion of the people in the choice of the legislature.

PART III: THE SIXTH PROTOCOL

Article 1

Abolition of the Death Penalty
The death penalty shall be abolished. No one shall be condemned to such penalty or executed.

Article 2

Death Penalty in Time of War
A State may make provision in its law for the death penalty in respect of acts committed in time of war or of imminent threat of war; such penalty shall be applied only in the instances laid down in the law and in accordance with its provisions. The State shall communicate to the Secretary General of the Council of Europe the relevant provisions of that law.

© Crown Copyright 1998

NOTES ON CONTRIBUTORS

Razia Karim is a solicitor. She joined the CRE in June 2000 as Senior Legal Policy Officer where she worked with colleagues on the implementation of the Race Relations (Amendment) Act 2000. Razia previously worked with Justice as a legal policy officer working on miscarriages of justice, discrimination and human rights.

Barbara Cohen is a solicitor. She was until recently Head of Legal Policy at the Commission for Racial Equality. Her previous legal experience includes working as a principal solicitor for a London local authority, as an assistant solicitor specialising in crime, discrimination and public law in a London legal aid firm and as legal officer at what was then the National Council for Civil Liberties.

Sharon Persaud is a solicitor and partner in the criminal department at Bindman & Partners. She regularly advises community-based groups and agencies, and has conducted seminars on the HRA for Rights of Women and Unison.

Philip Engelman is a barrister at Cloisters. He practises in the fields of public law, commercial law and employment law. He is particularly interested in education with many reported cases in this area. He is the author of *Commercial Judicial Review* (Sweet & Maxwell, 2001) and a contributing author to *Bullen & Leake & Jacobs* (Sweet & Maxwell, 2001) on education.

Ramby de Mello is a barrister at 6 King's Bench Walk.

Judith Farbey is a barrister at Tooks Court Chambers, where she specialises in immigration and asylum law. She is a member of the Executive Committee of the Immigration Law Practitioners' Association and a member of the Immigration Services Commissioner's Advisory Panel. She has been a visiting lecturer to the course 'Working with Refugee Families' at the Tavistock Clinic (London) since 1996.

Geoffrey Bindman is a solicitor, and senior partner of Bindman & Partners.

He is also visiting professor of law at University College, London; honorary president of the Discrimination Law Association; chairman of the Society of Labour Lawyers; and formerly Legal Adviser to the Commission for Racial Equality and Equal Opportunities Commission.

Makbool Javaid is a solicitor and partner in employment law at law firm DLA. He was formerly head of litigation at the Commission for Racial Equality.

Stephen Simblet is a barrister at 2 Garden Court Chambers, specialising in civil liberties law. He undertakes judicial review work in community care and mental health law, and has been in a number of reported decisions in those areas. He is an Editor of the *Community Care Law Reports*, published by Legal Action.

Rajiv Menon is a barrister at 2 Garden Court Chambers. He specialises in criminal defence and civil actions against the police. He was junior counsel to Duwayne Brooks during the Stephen Lawrence Inquiry.

Heather Williams is a barrister at Doughty Street Chambers. She specialises in discrimination law and claims against the police. She has appeared in a number of reported cases concerning discrimination law. She is a member of the Discrimination Law Association, the Police Actions Lawyers Group and the Housing Law Practitioners' Association, and is a regular lecturer.

Sadiq Khan is a solicitor and partner in Christian Fisher Khan solicitors. He is Chair of Liberty and vice-chair of the Legal Action Group. He is a Councillor in a London local authority where he sits on both the Police Consultative Committee and Racial Incidents Panel. He has given oral evidence to the Home Office Select Committee on police misconduct and discipline and was a Member of the Advisory Committee of Liberty examining an independent police complaints system in 1999/2000. He is a visiting lecturer at the University of North London.

Barry Clarke is a solicitor and partner with Russell Jones & Walker, specialising in employment, discrimination and human rights law, acting predominantly for trade unions and their members. He is a member of the Law Society's International Human Rights Committee, the Discrimination Law Association, the Industrial Law Society and the Society of Labour Lawyers. He is on the management committee of the Employment Lawyers Association.

Helena Cook is currently a freelance consultant in international human rights and public law and a member of the Legal Services Commission's Regional Legal Services Committee for London. Formerly head of Amnesty International's Legal Office and Director of Policy and Research of the Public Law Project, she has also taught international human rights law at the Universities of Essex and Nottingham. She has written a number of pieces on contemporary human rights and public law issues in various books and journals and is a member of the Board of Directors of Interights.

Veena Vasista is currently working as Program Associate dealing with racial discrimination at the International Human Rights Law Group in Washington D.C. She was formerly Human Rights Programme Coordinator for the 1990 Trust. In both capacities she has been working to raise awareness about racism as a violation of human rights and to facilitate the participation of racial, ethnic and religious minority groups in international human rights fora. While at the 1990 Trust, she was an active member of the UK Human Rights Task Force, set up to assist public authorities in implementing the Human Rights Act.

Chris Myant is a journalist. He is currently senior media officer at the CRE.

INDEX